Cat Country
Old Country Road Vol. 2

Jose A. Villalba

This Book is dedicated to all my family and friends who have always supported and inspired my art and creativity. JV

The images in this book are all original hand drawings by me; I did not use any digital tools to create them. I tend to like the more handmade look when it comes to drawings and coloring books. This book is a cat lovers dream it features 21 original drawings of cats in country settings; basically doing whatever cats like to do.

Some of the drawings have also been printed in a smaller size for more enjoyment and provide a challenge for the more experienced colorist. I have also included 6 practice pages featuring the cats in this book, these practice pages will let you try out different color schemes on the cats before you start coloring the main pages.

We suggest that the colorist use some sort of backing like cardboard when coloring to prevent bleed through, especially when using markers.

If you have any questions or wish to contact me do so at:

JVillalba1970@hotmail.com

JVCreative@hotmail.com

You can also message me and check out more of my projects and artwork at:

Facebook, look for JVCretive artist.

On Etsy at JVCreative.

Thank you for your support……..and keep coloring. JV
Look for my other books, Old Country Road, and Aztec and Mayan inspired designs.

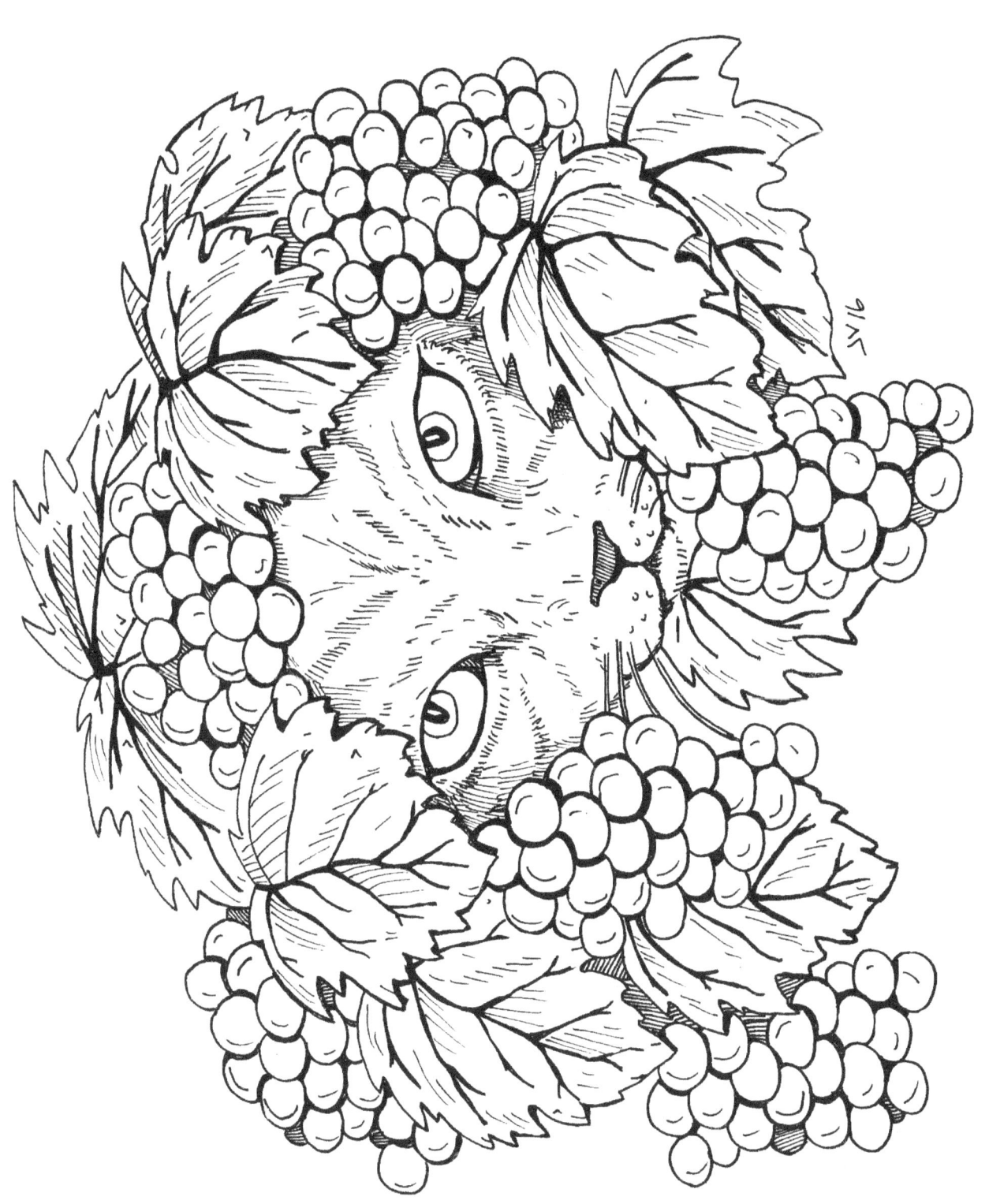

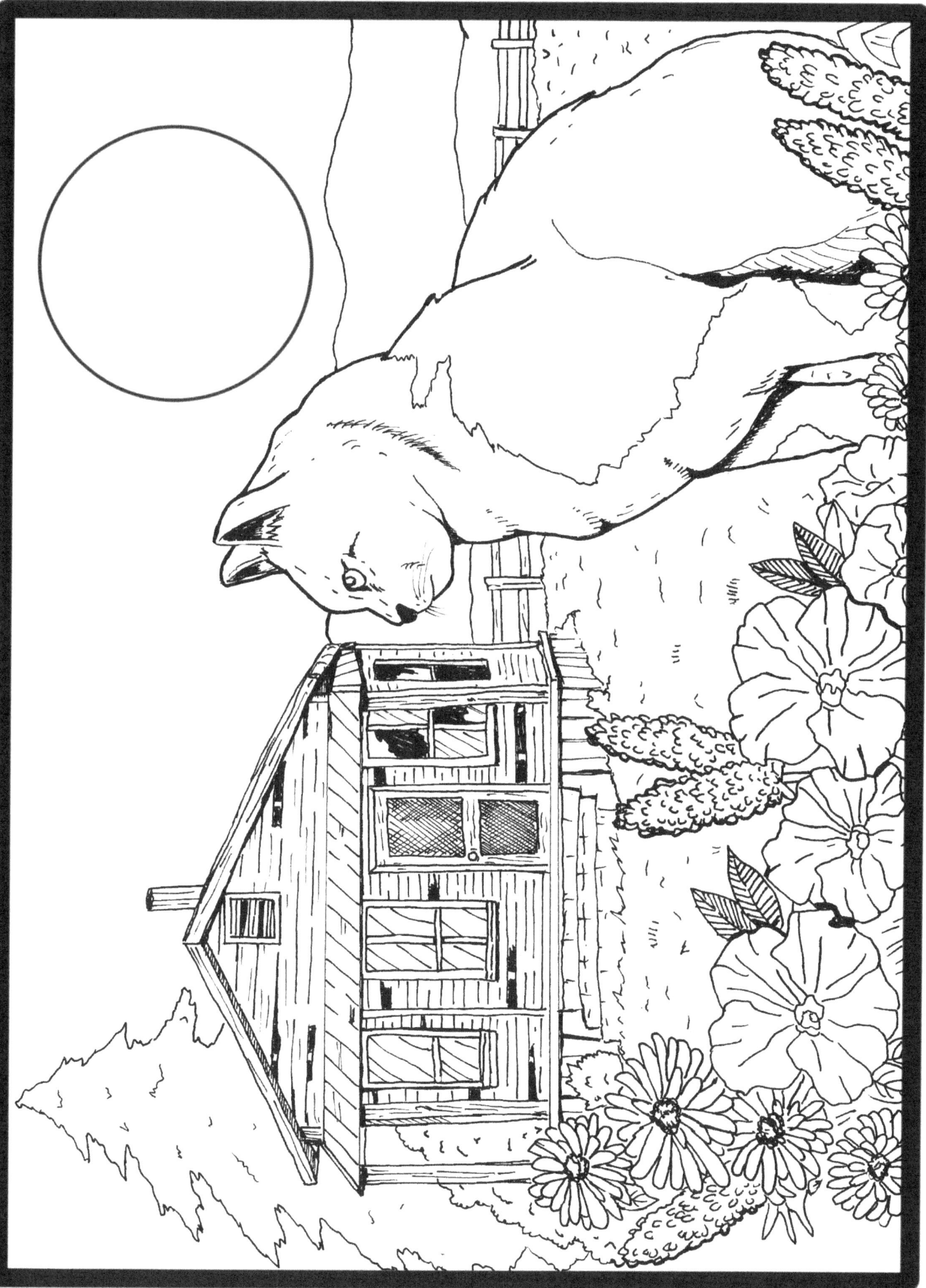

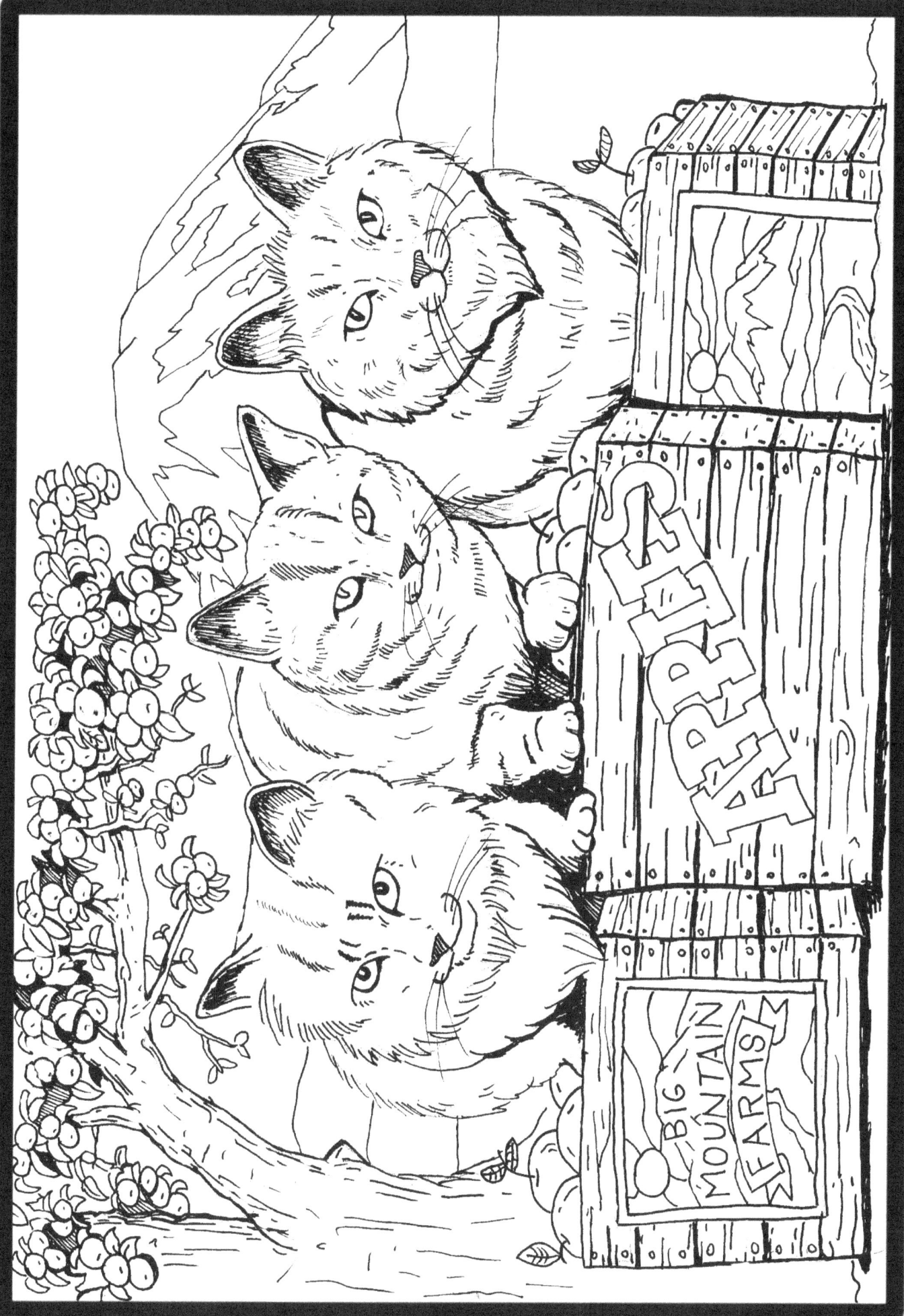

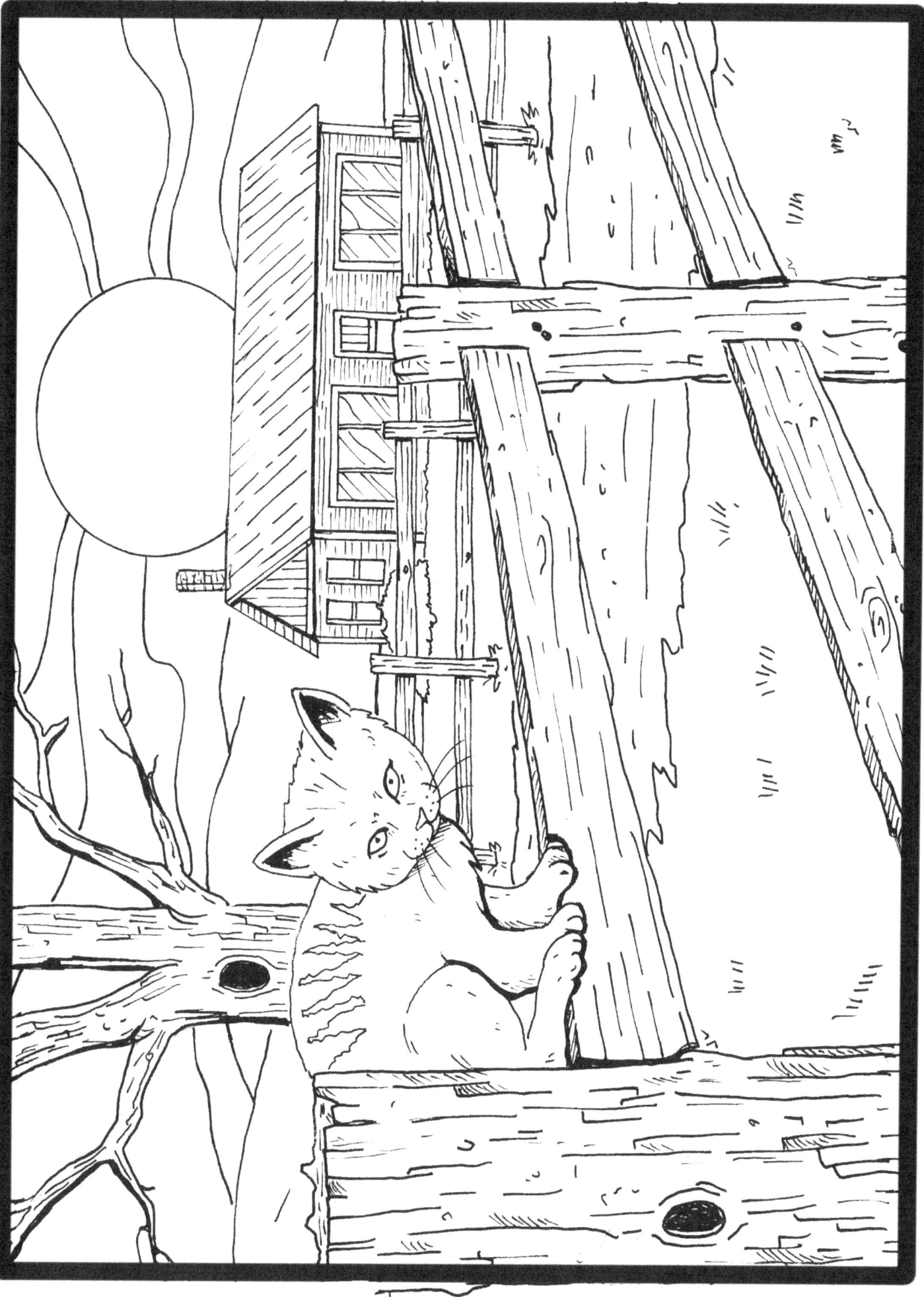

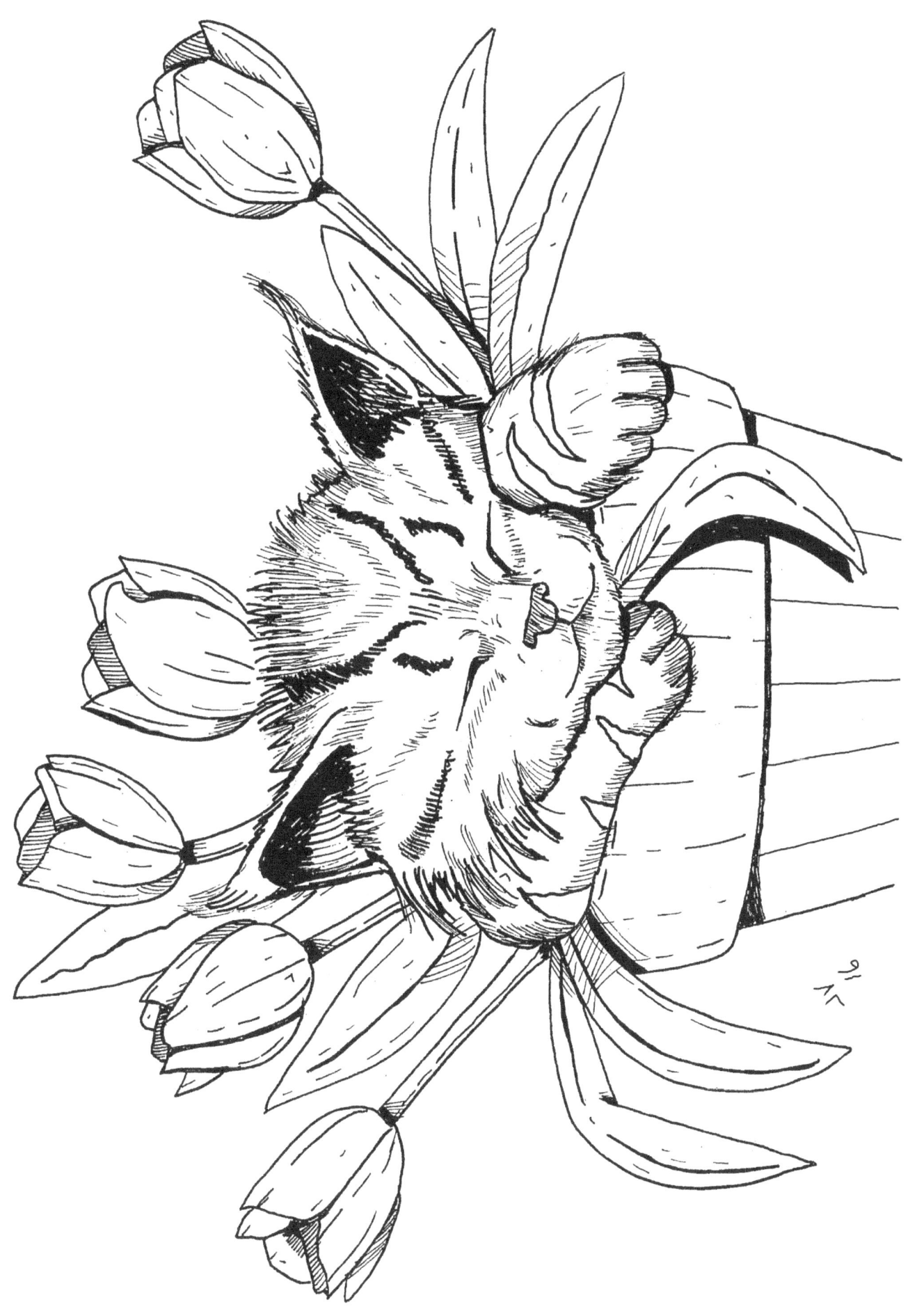

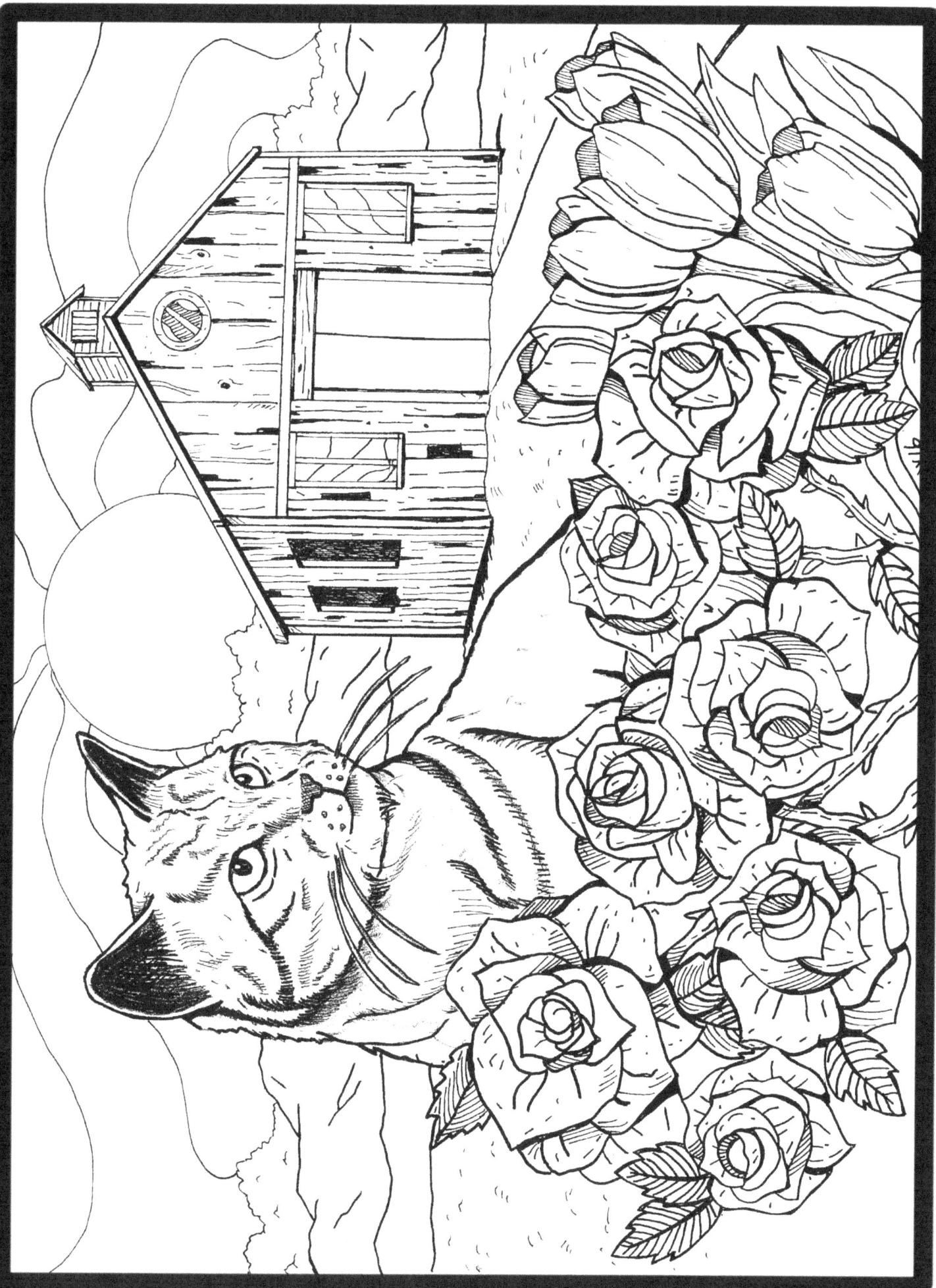

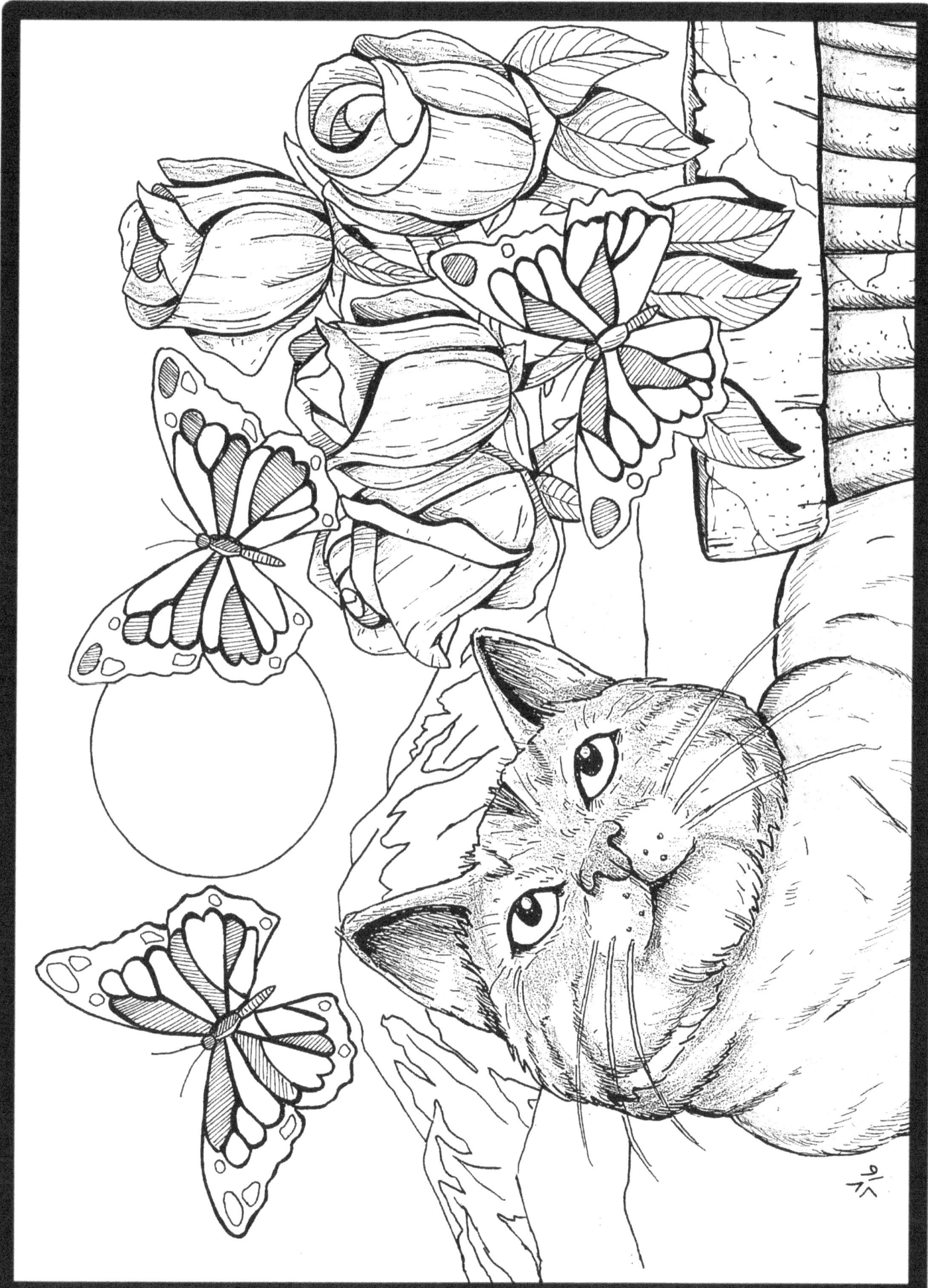

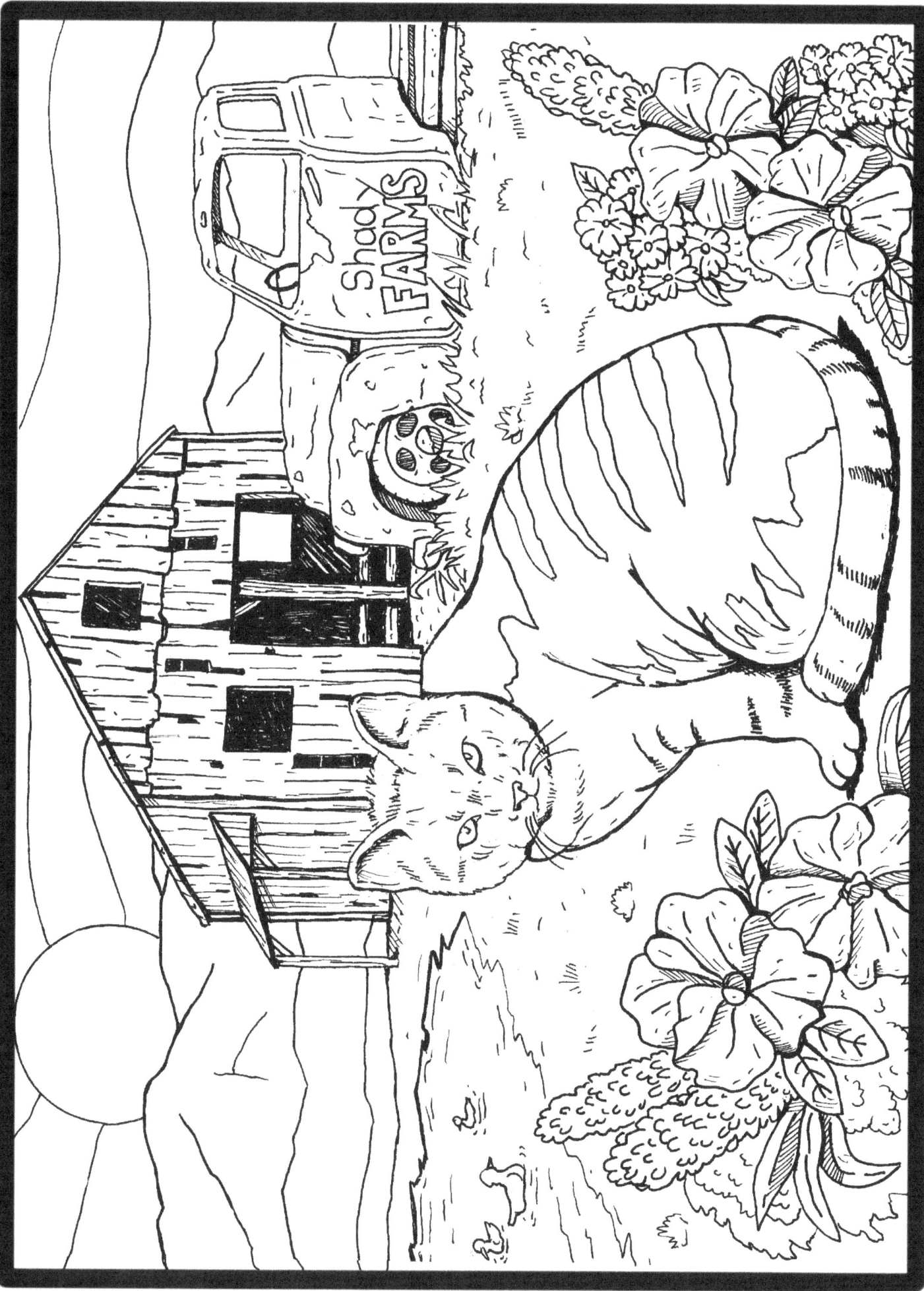

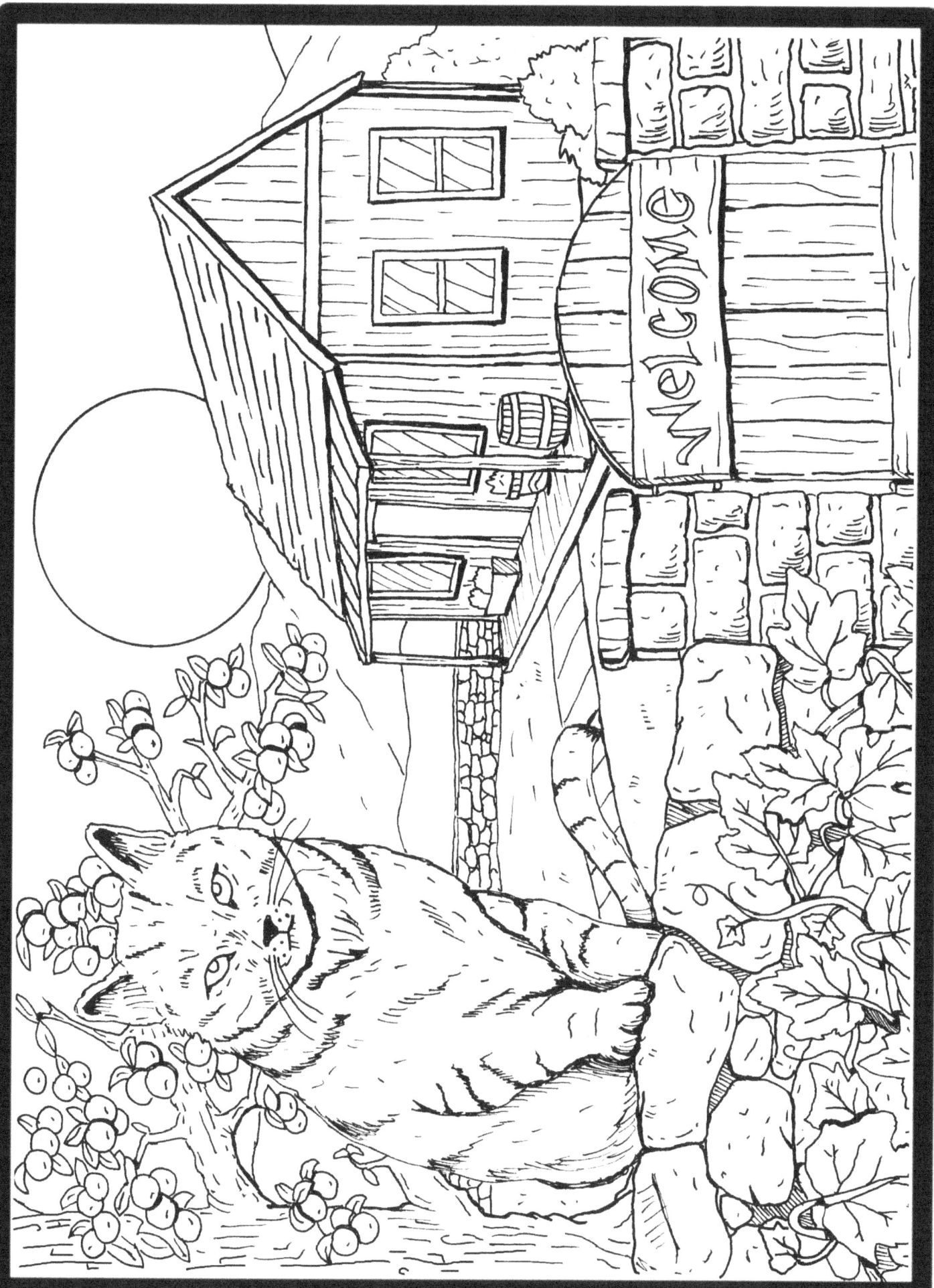

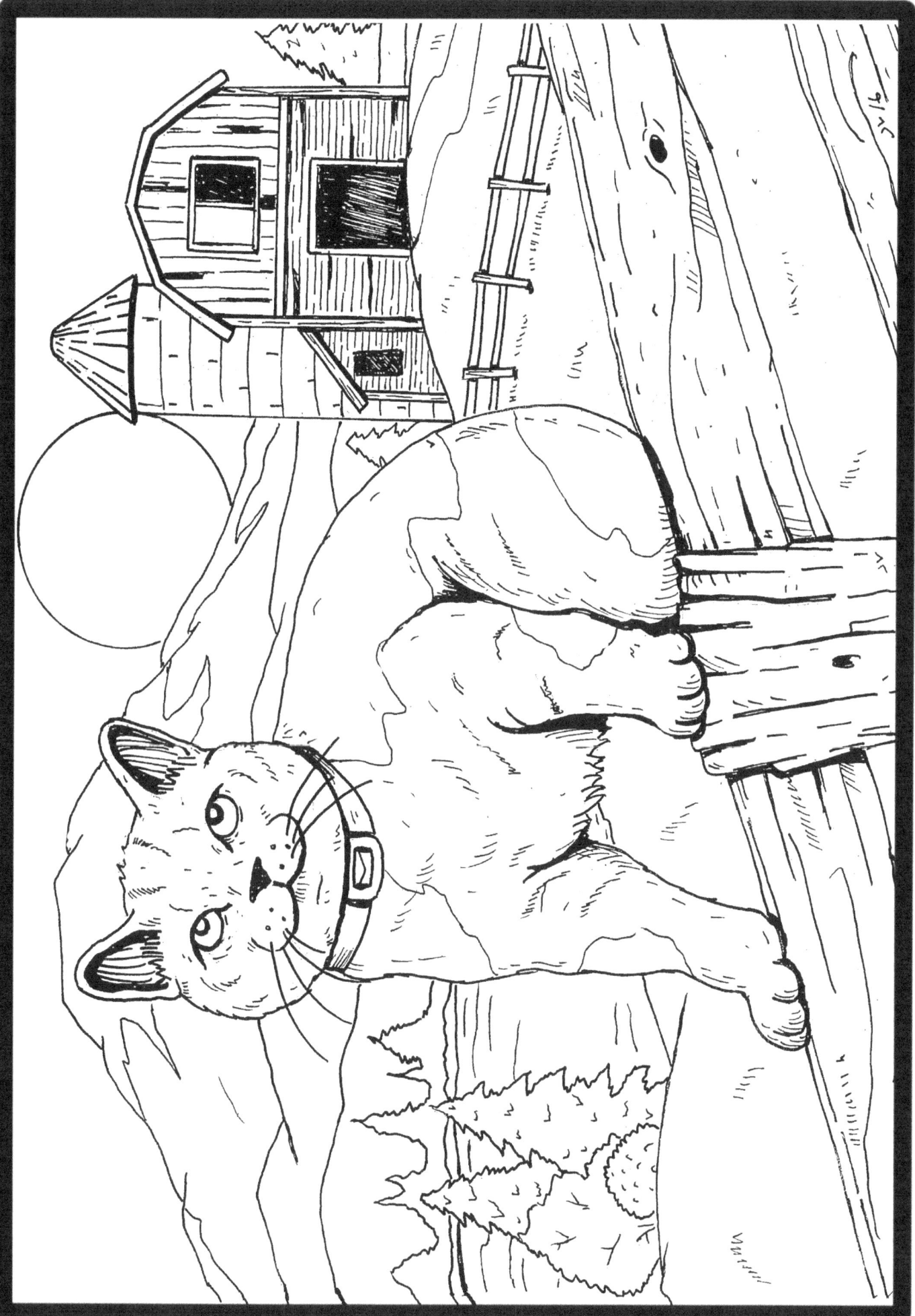

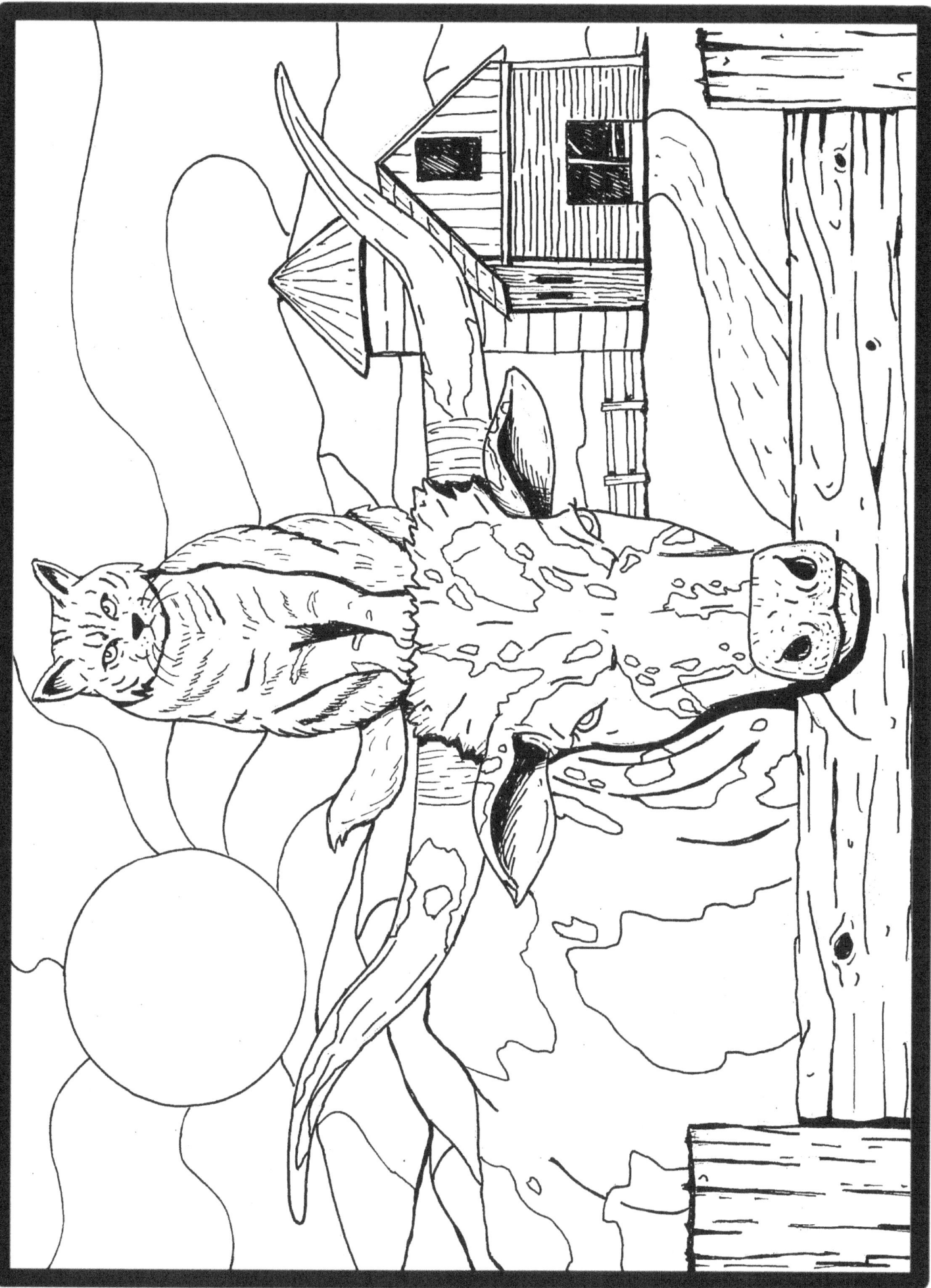

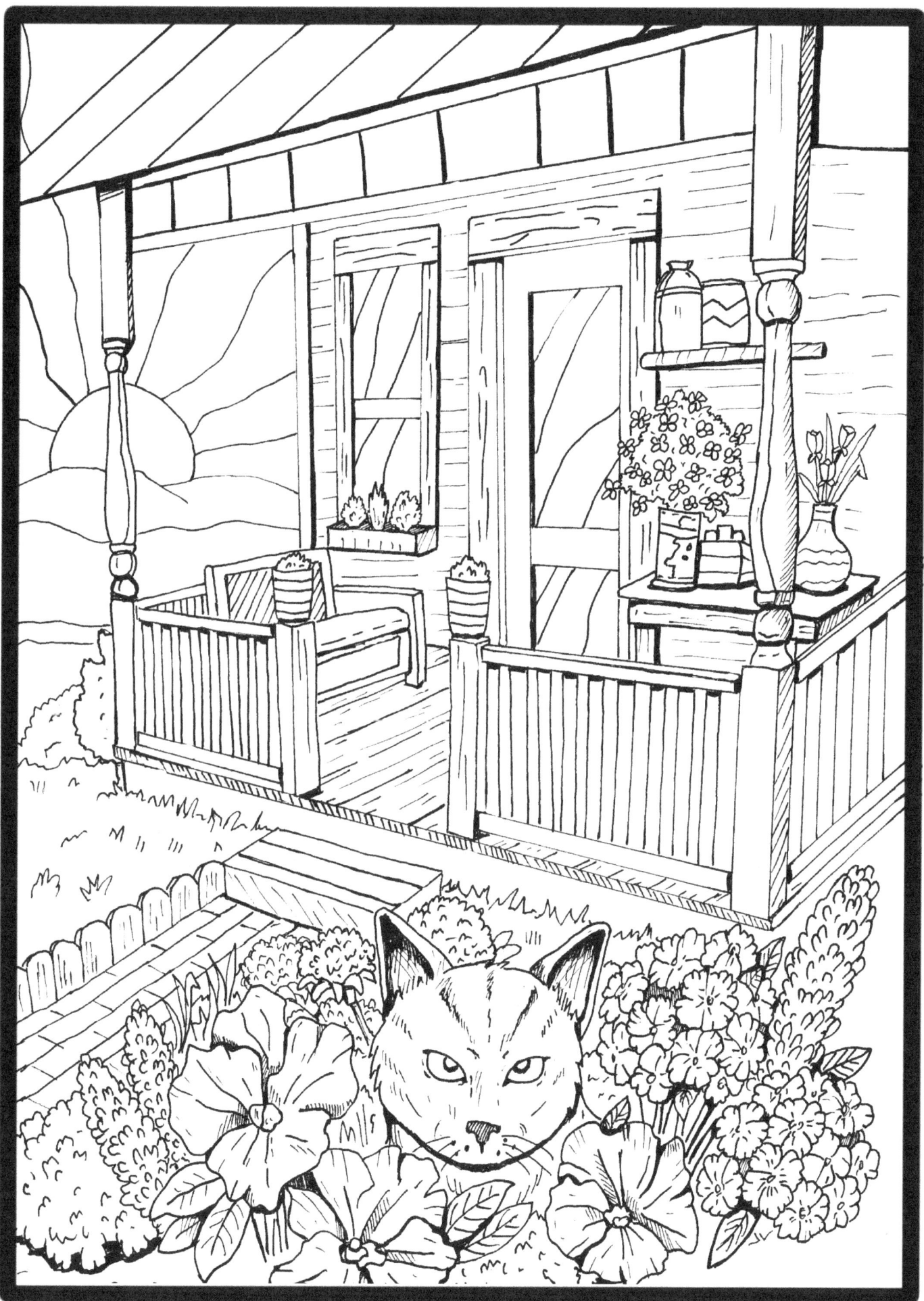

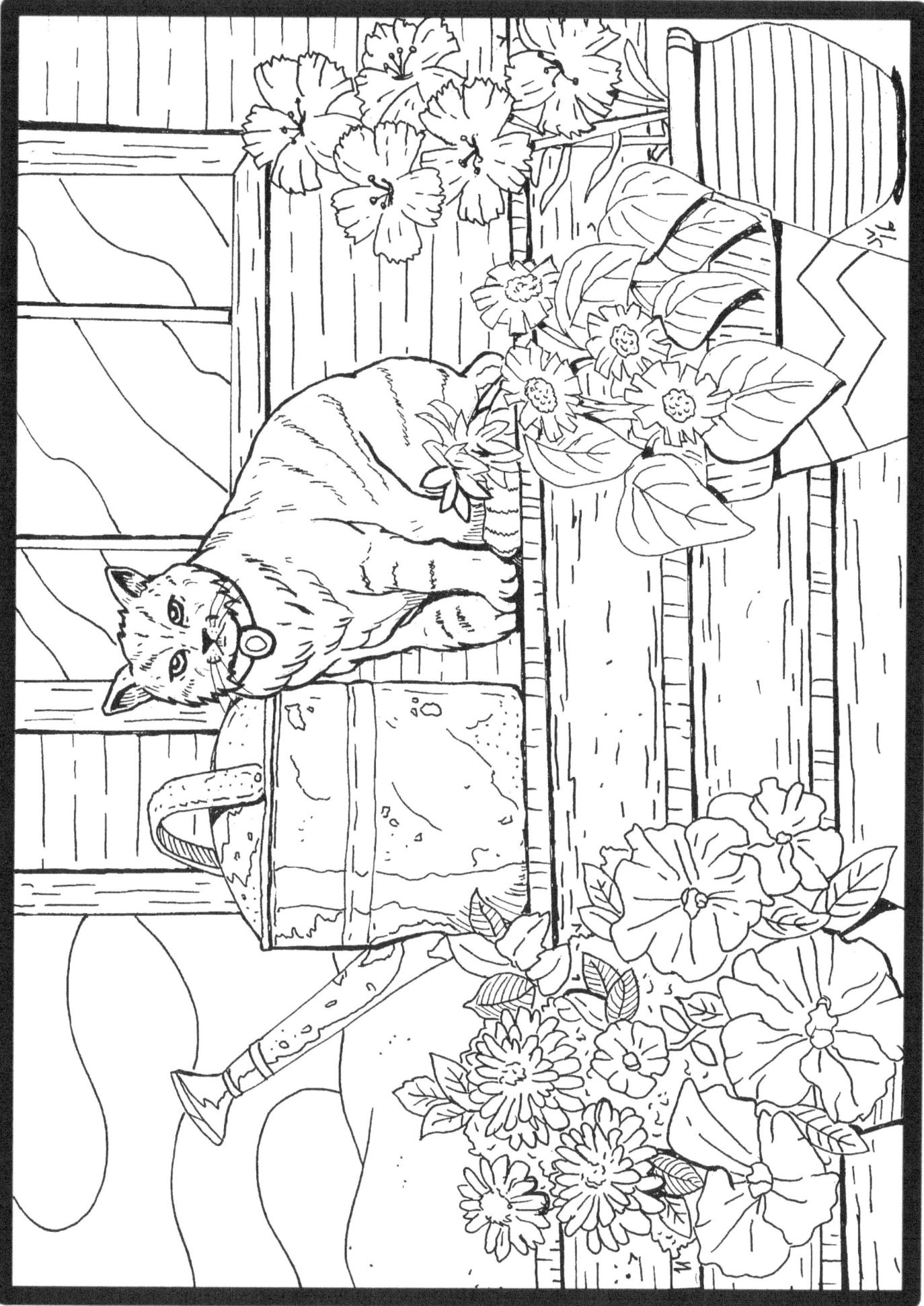

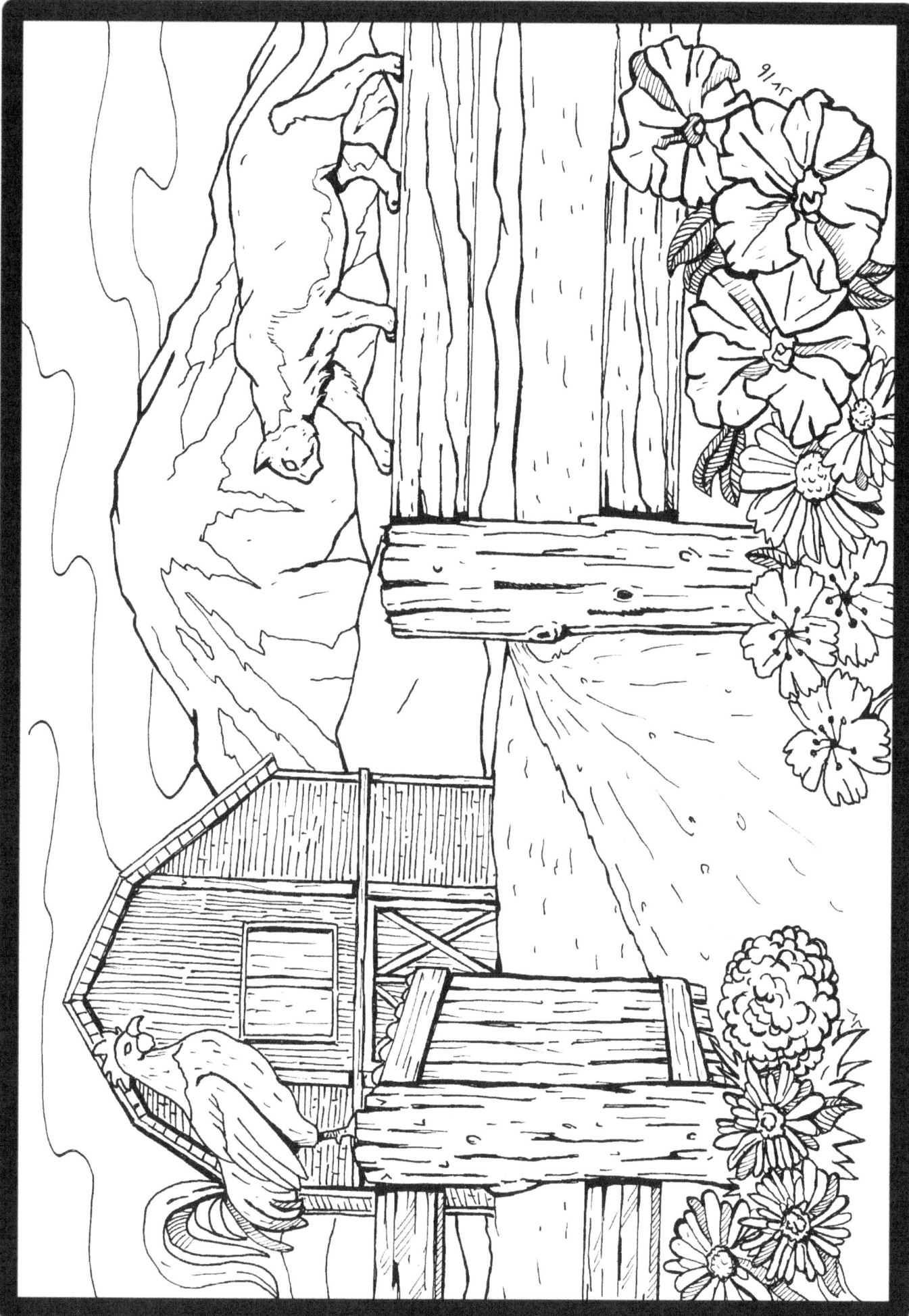

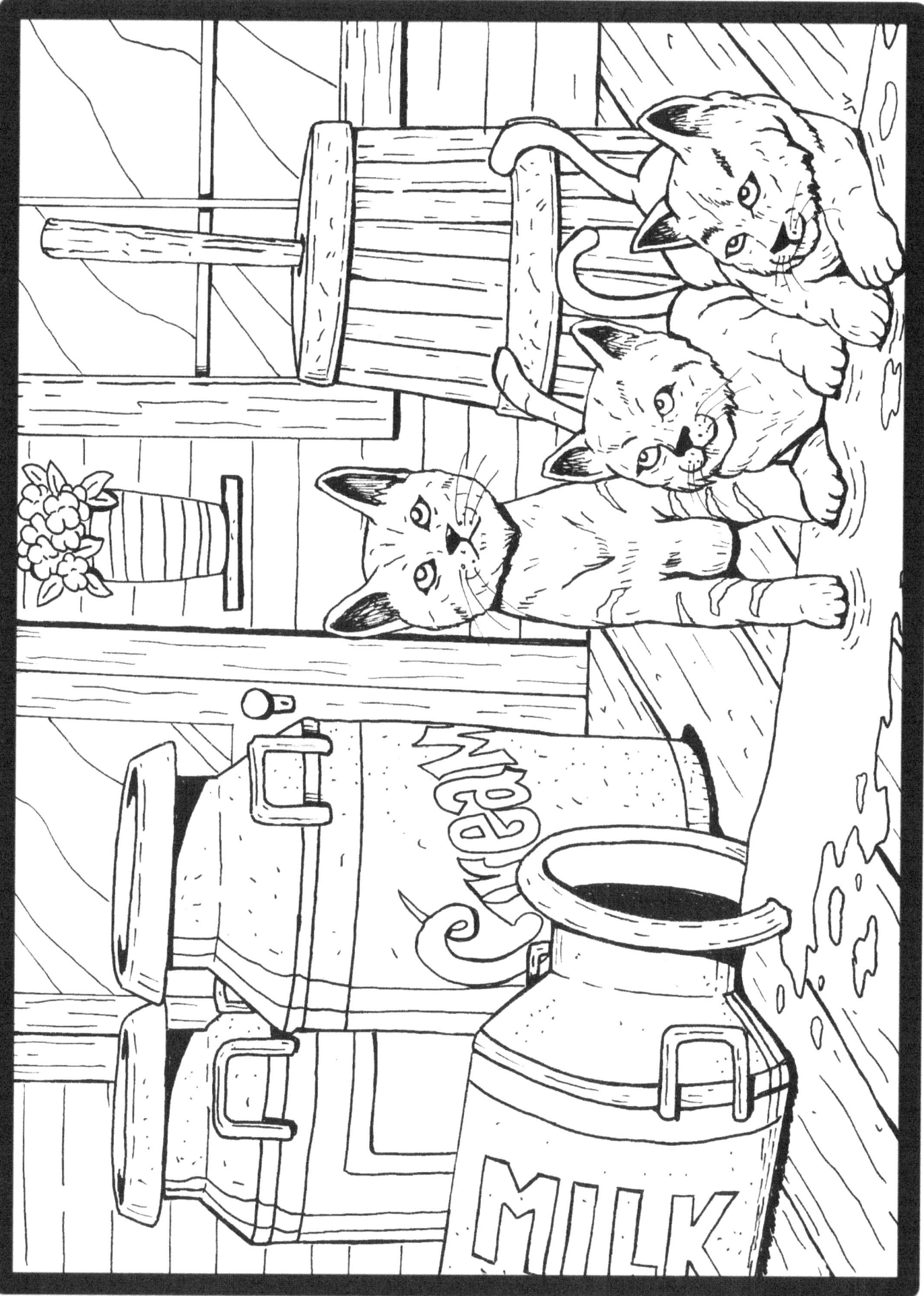

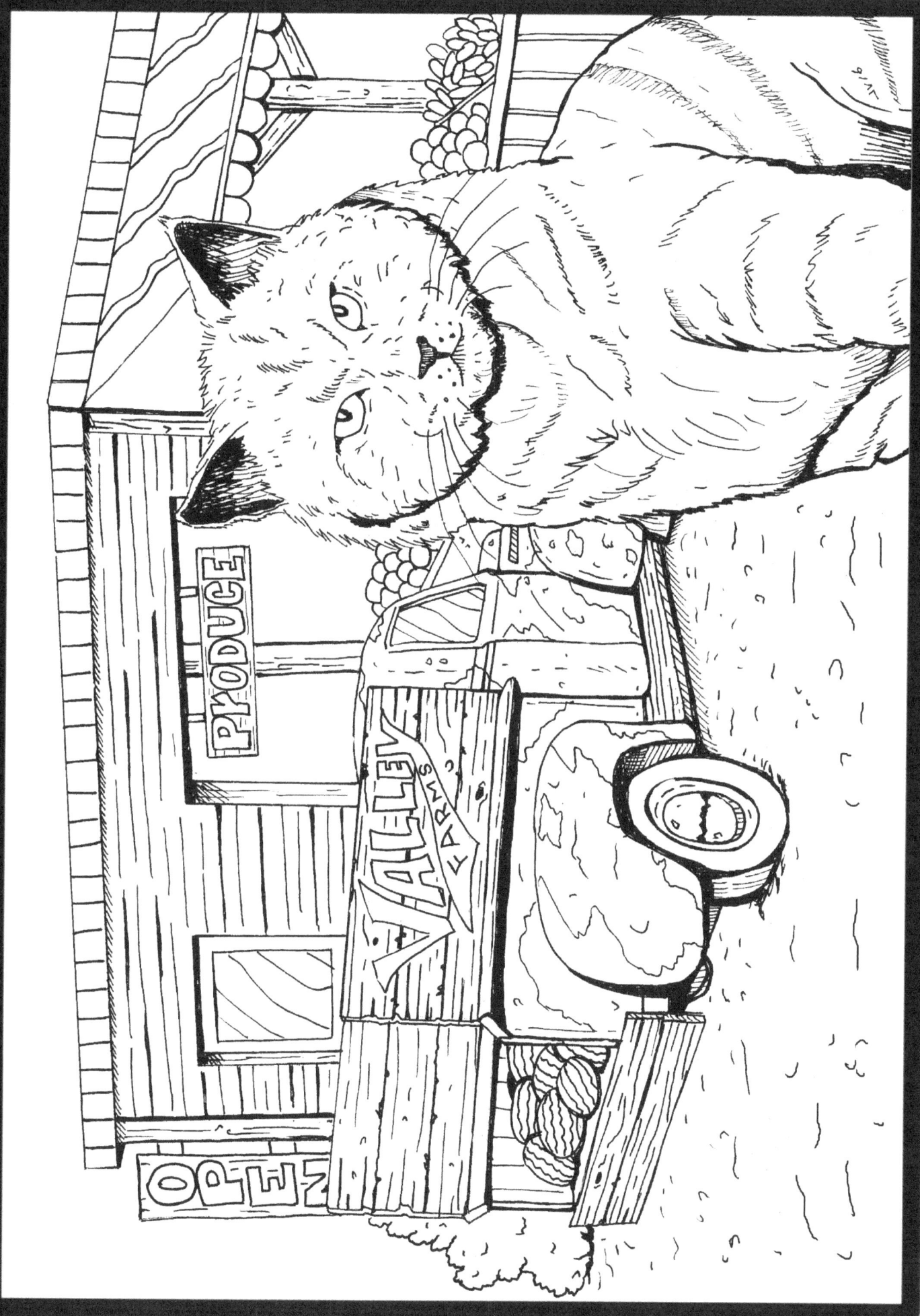

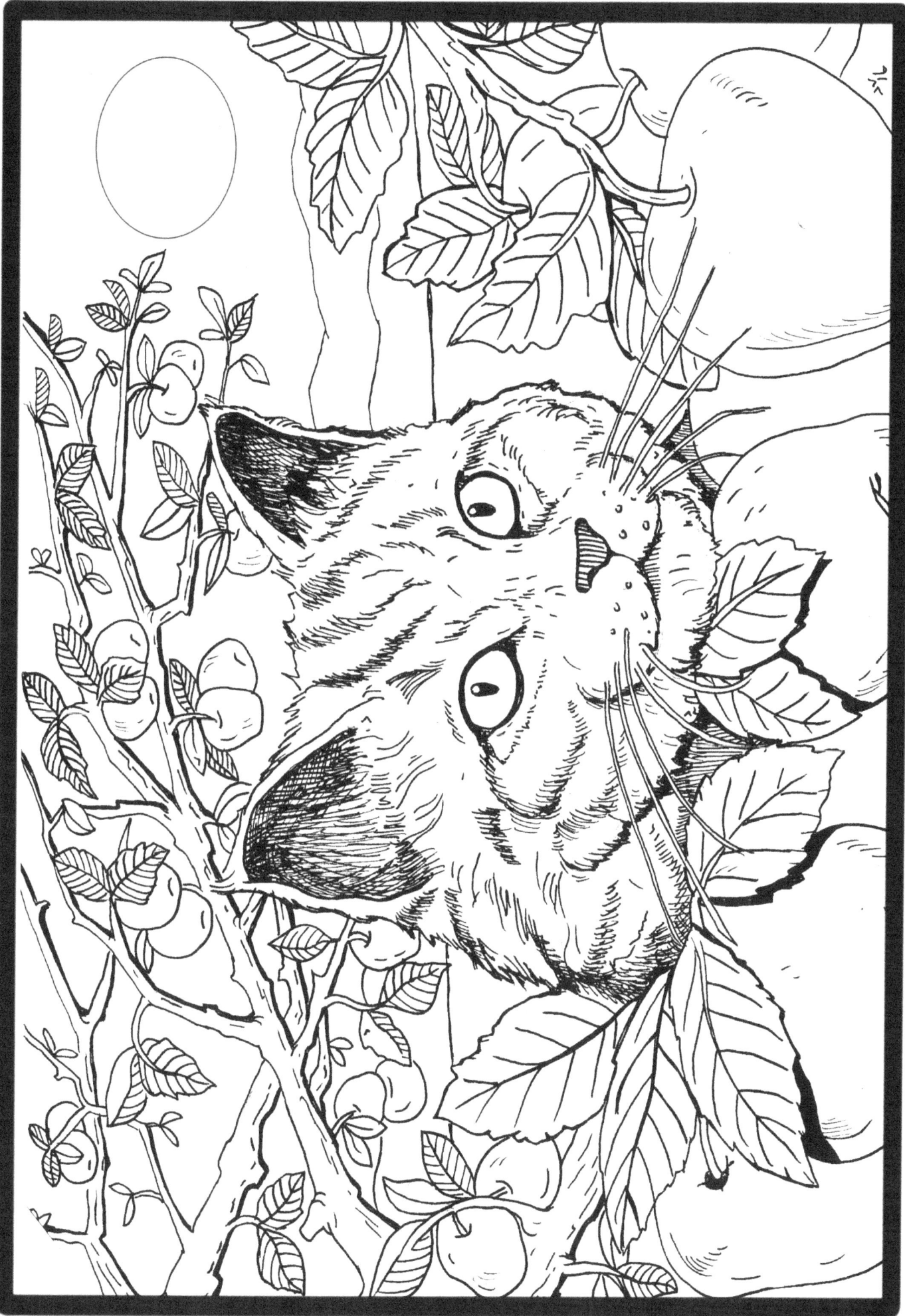

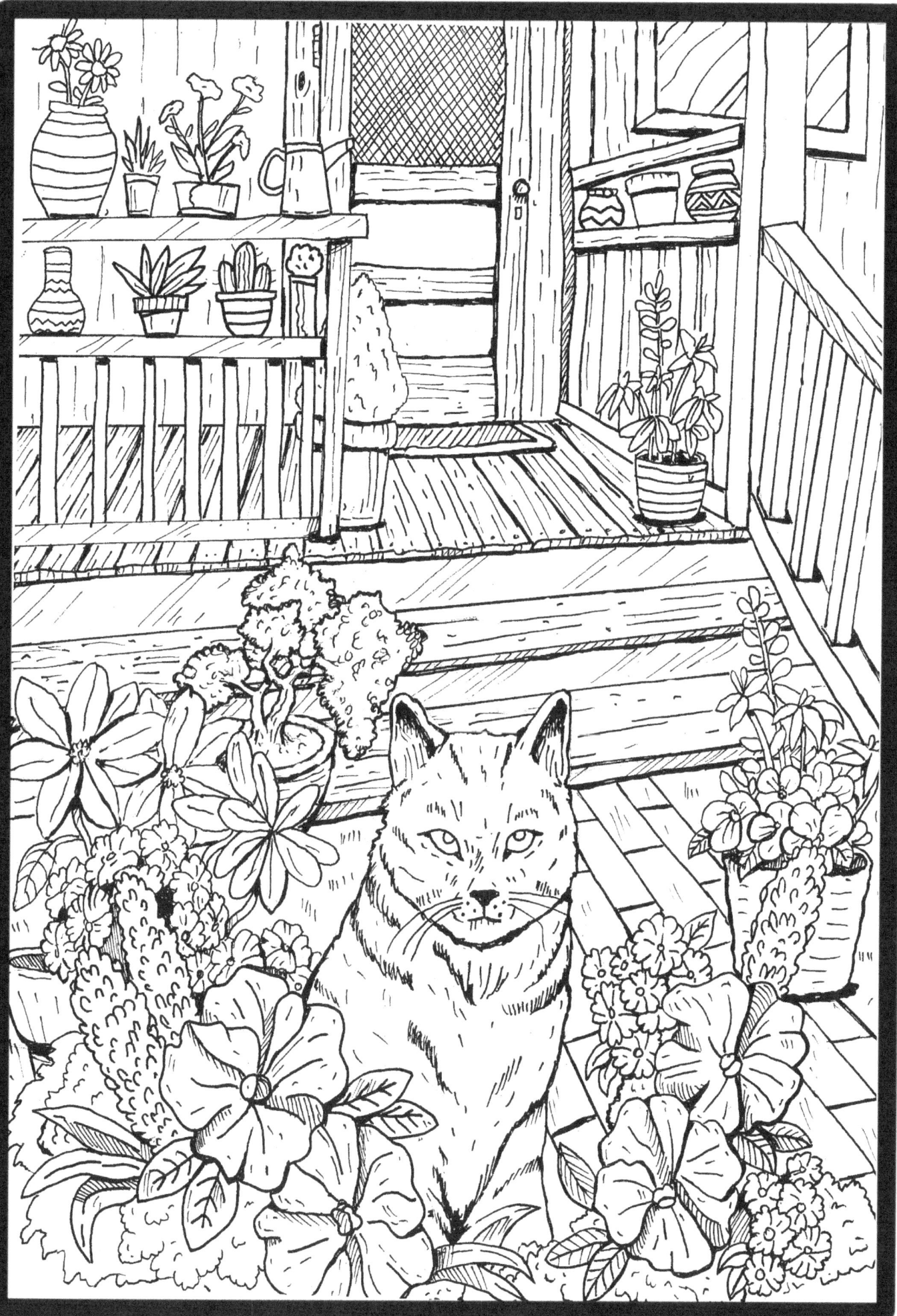

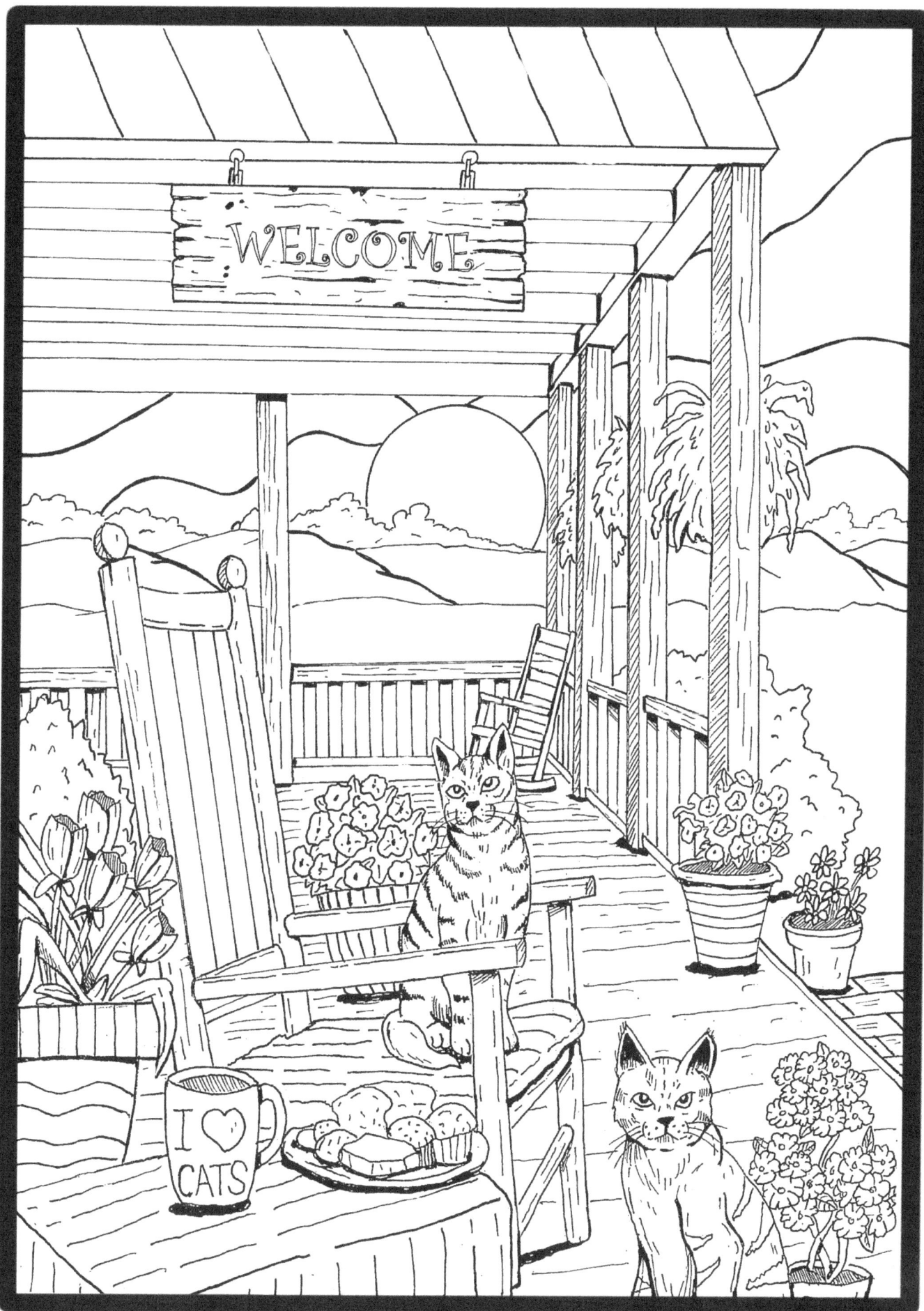

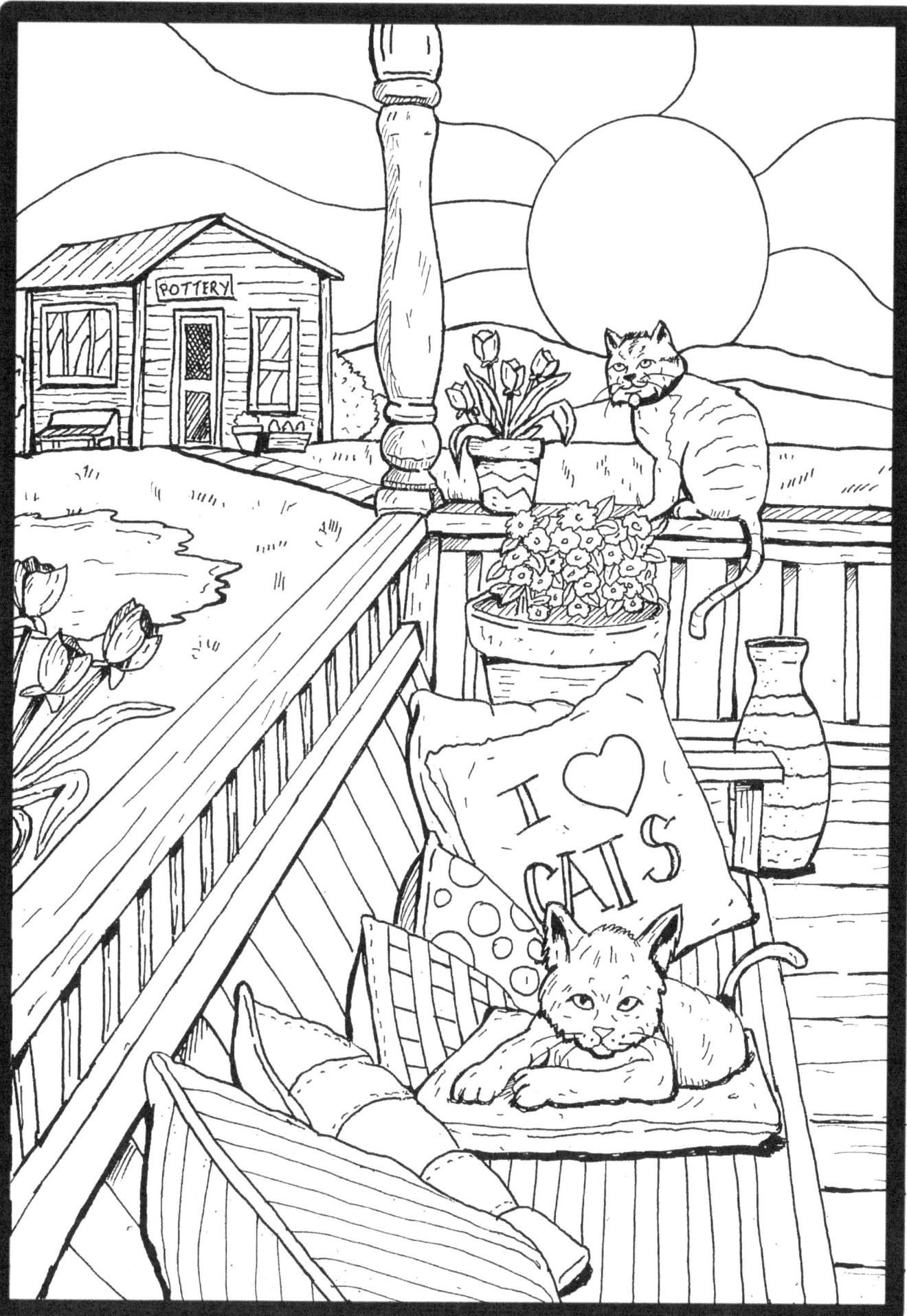

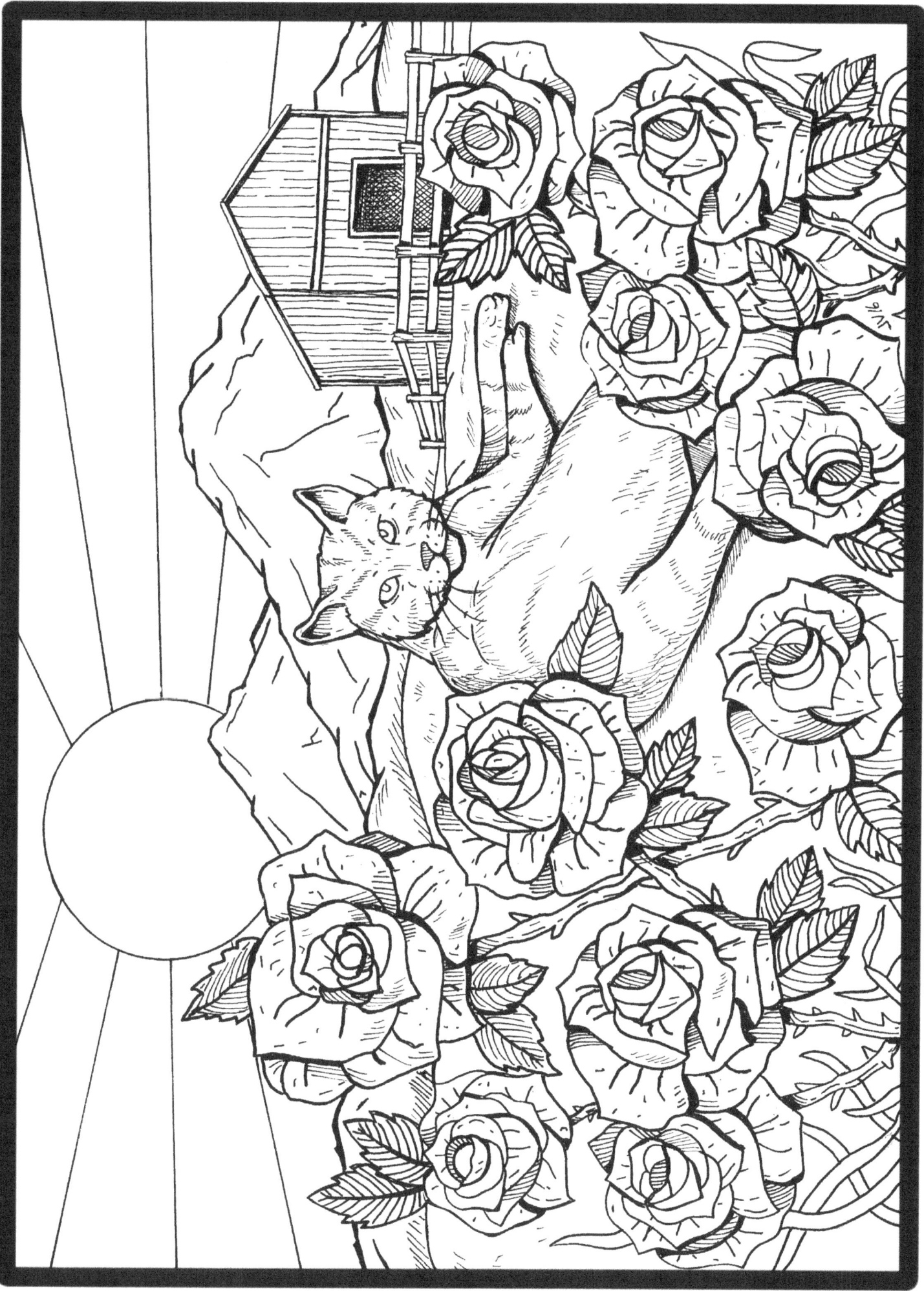

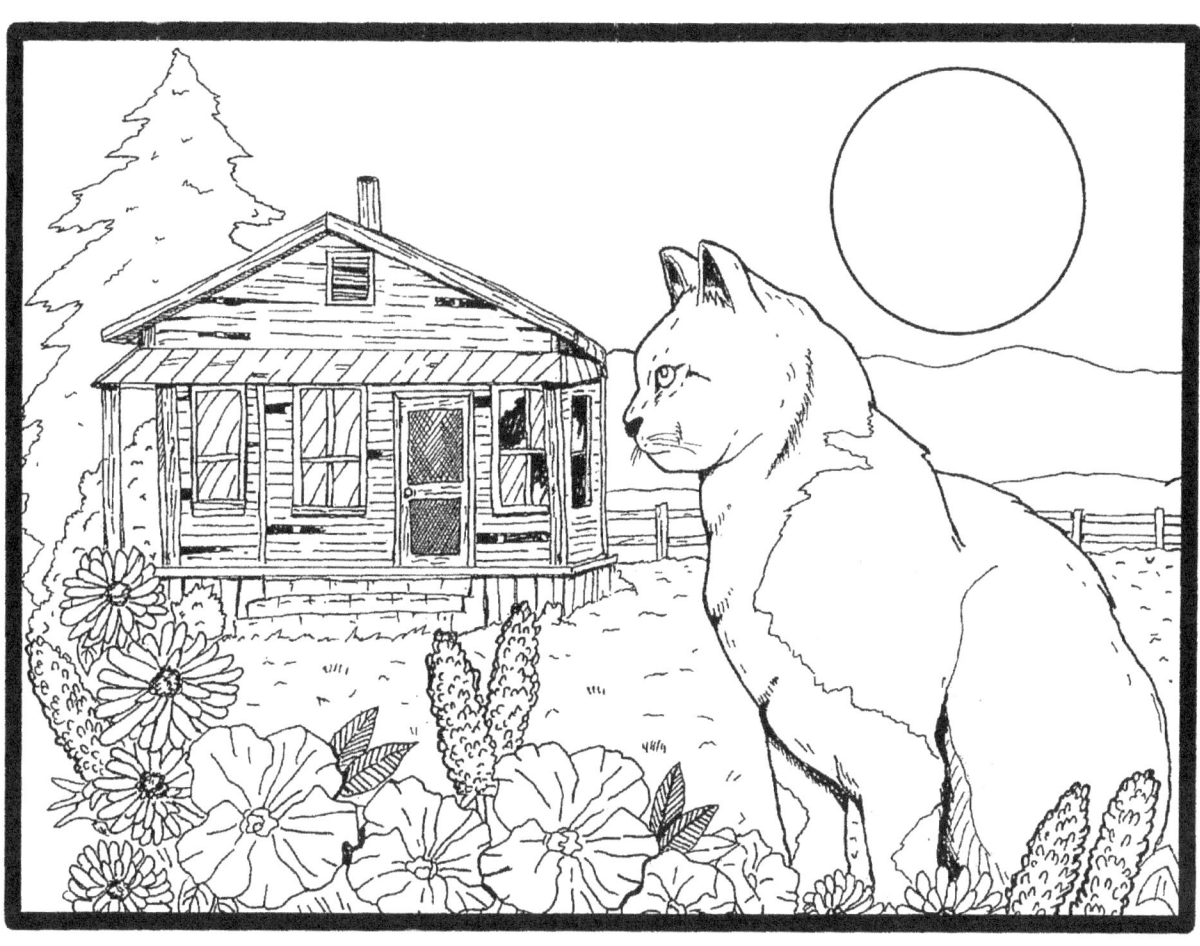

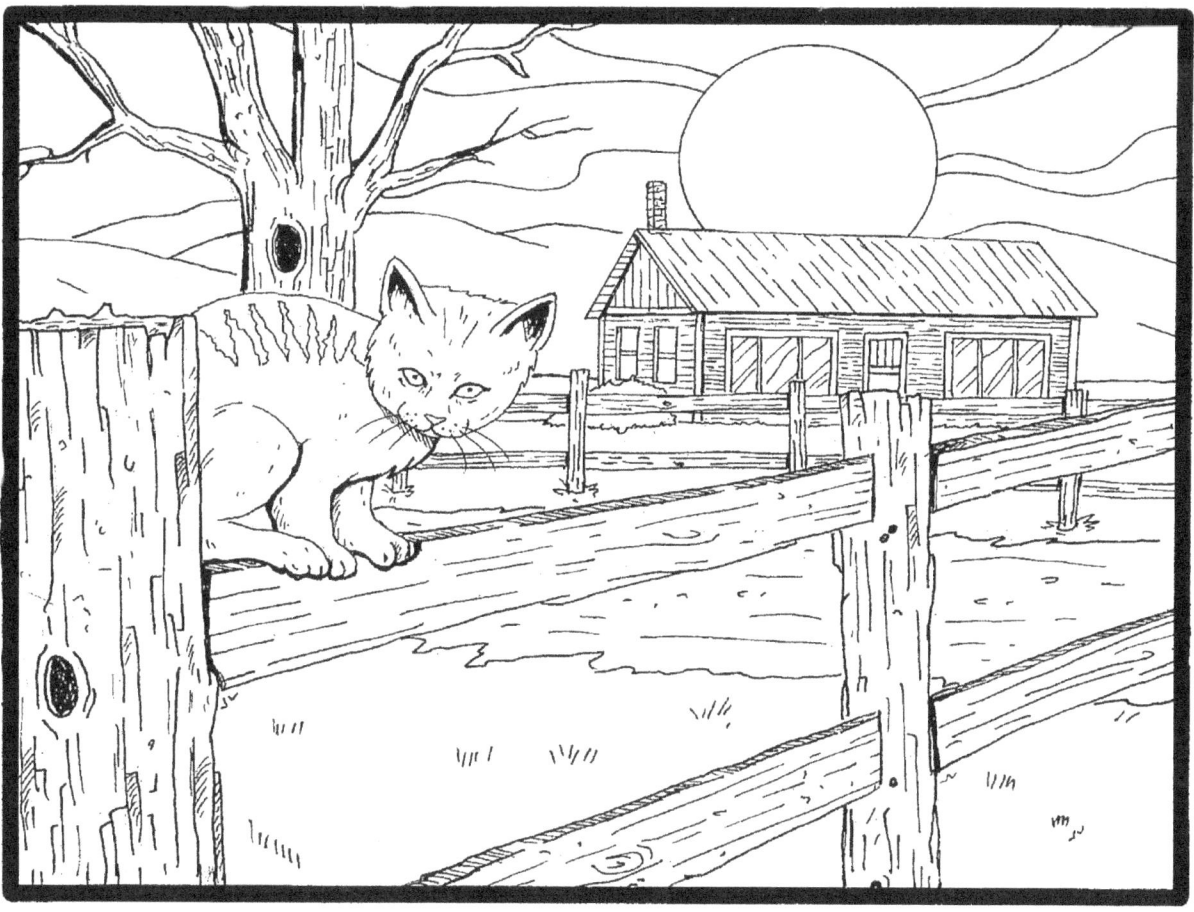

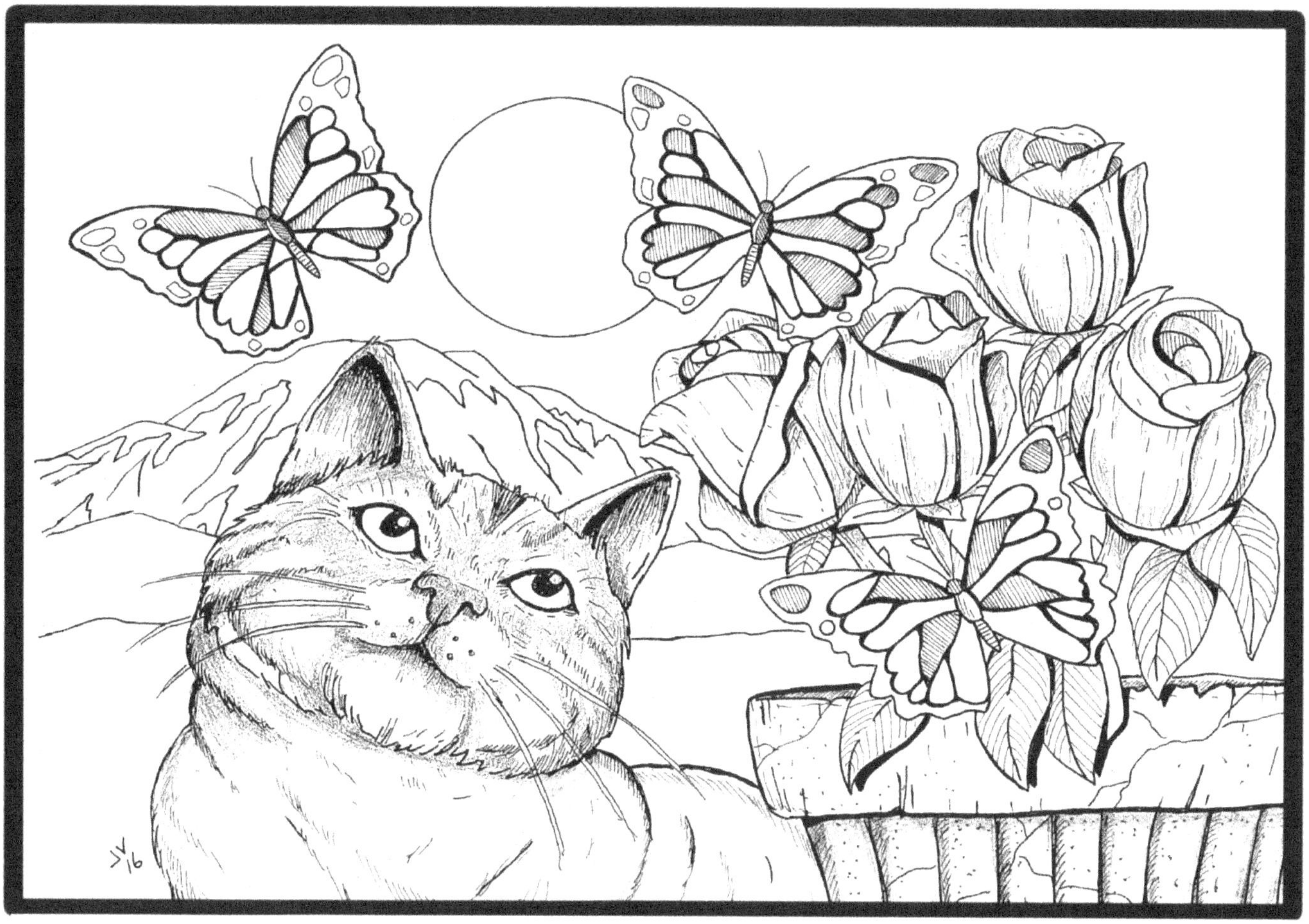

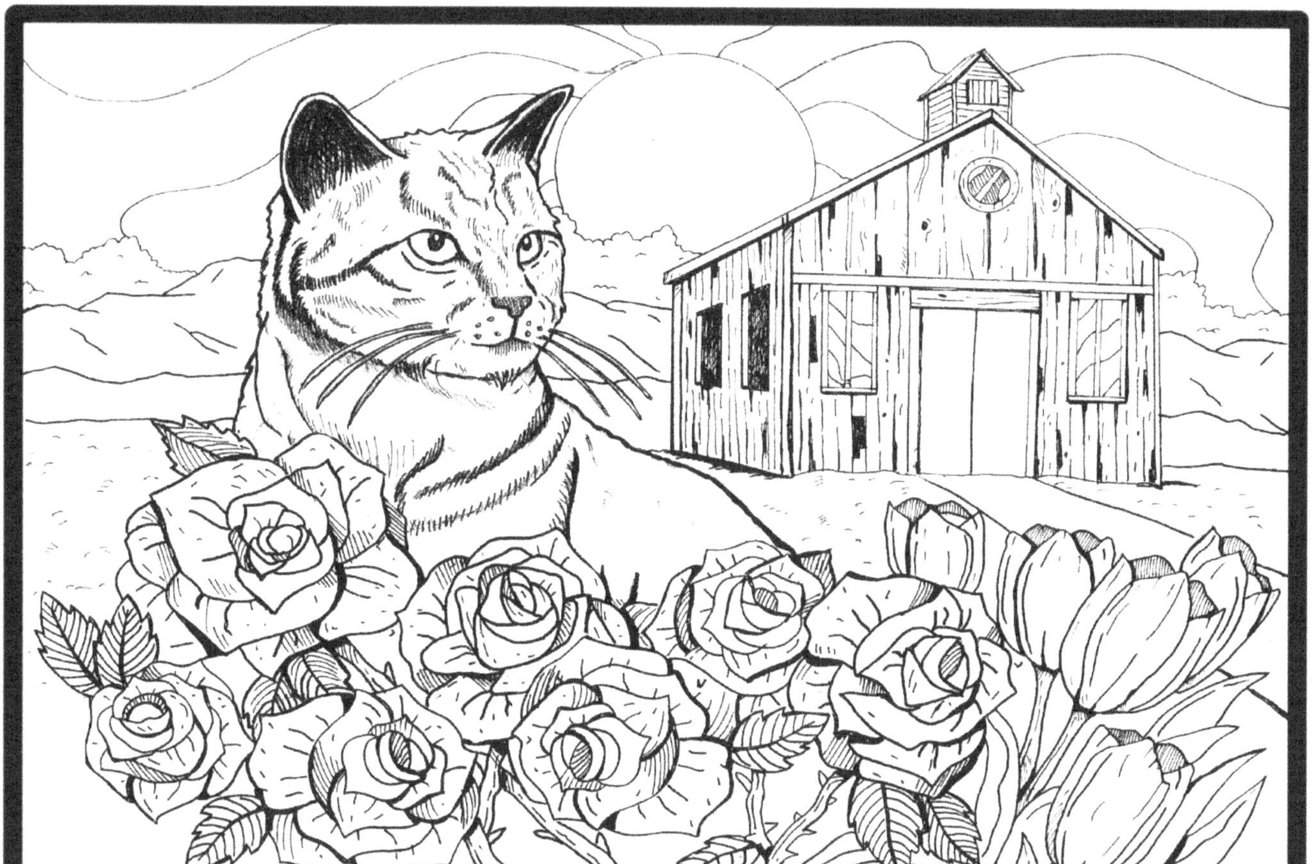

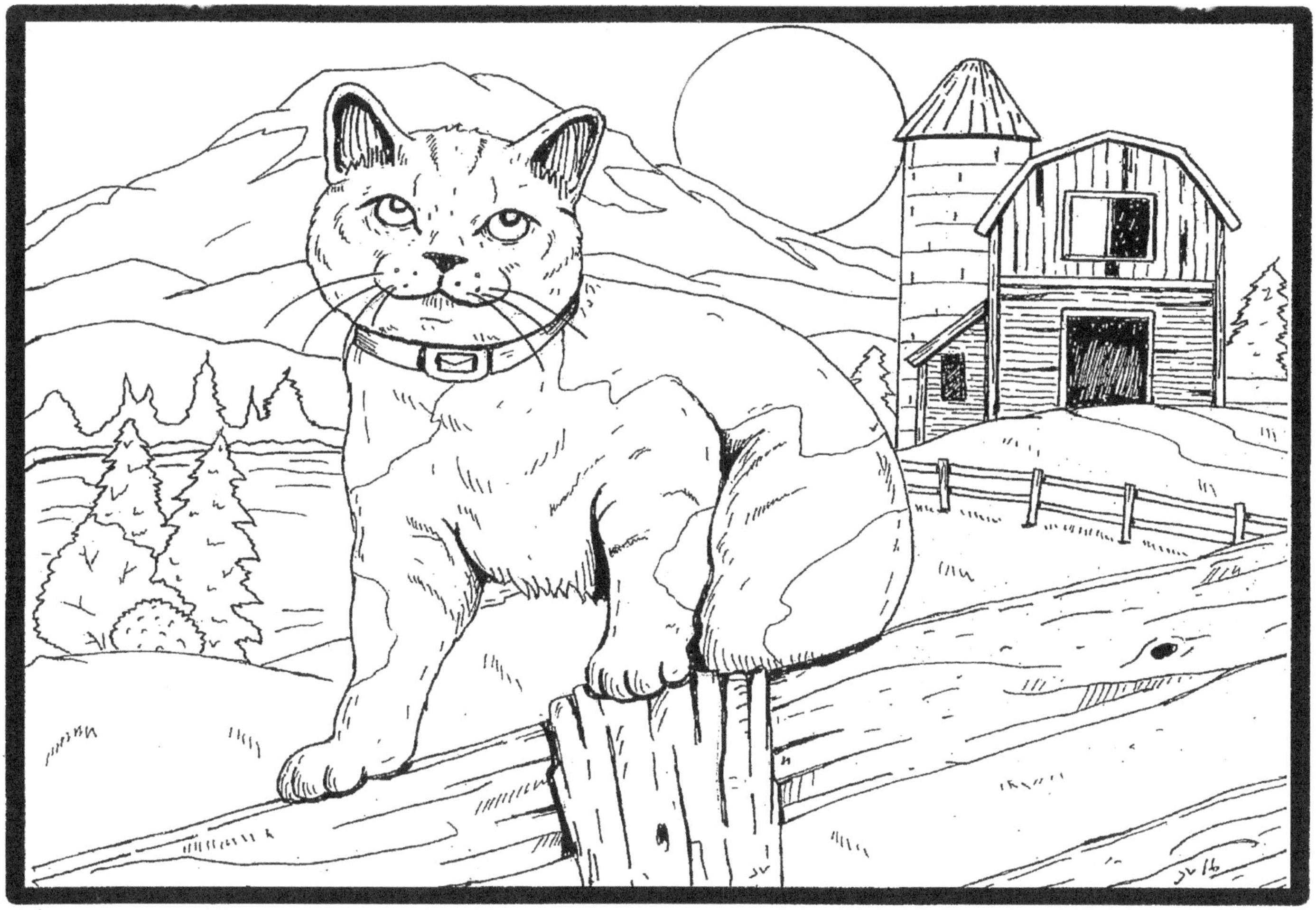

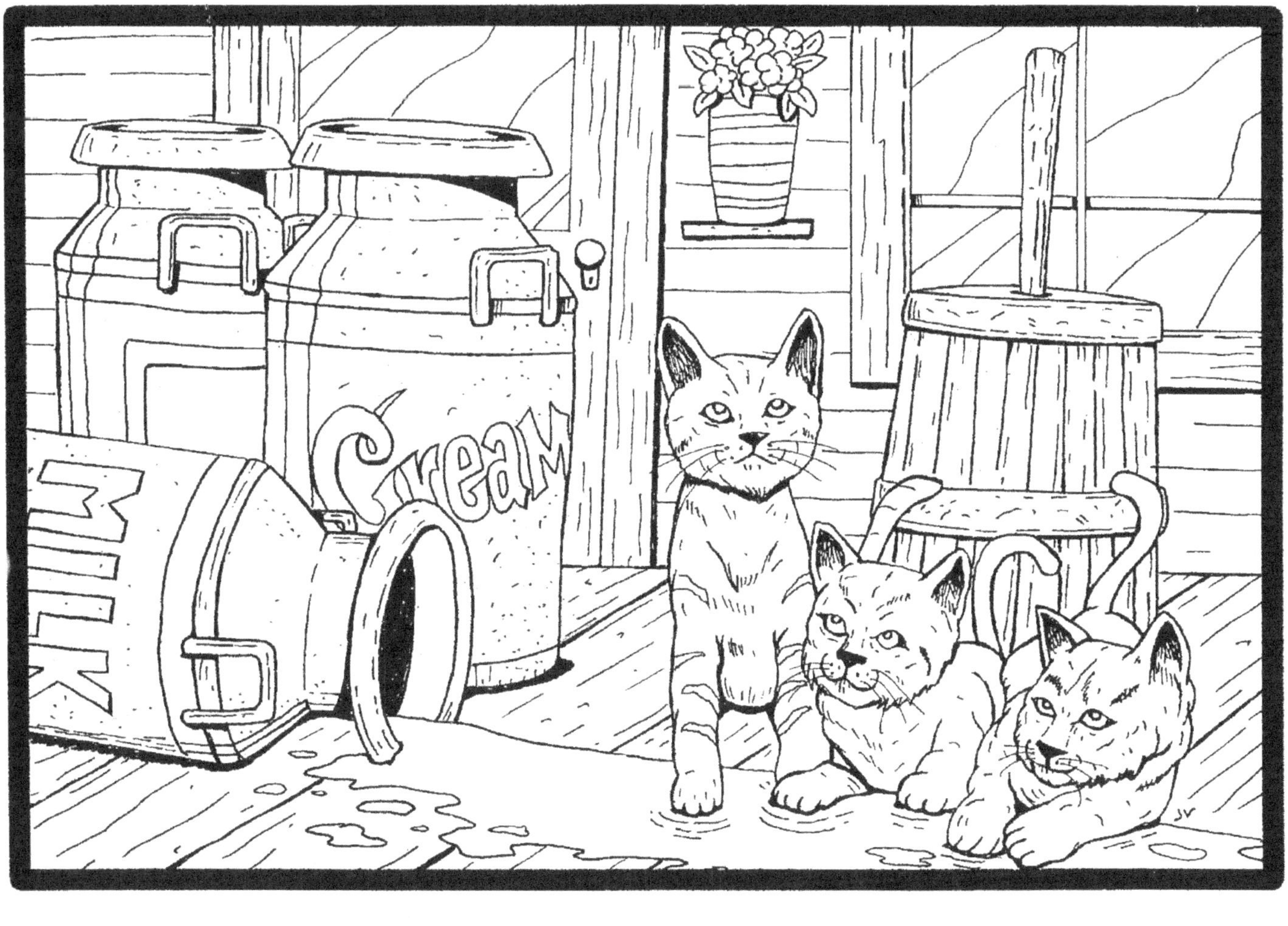
Cream
MILK

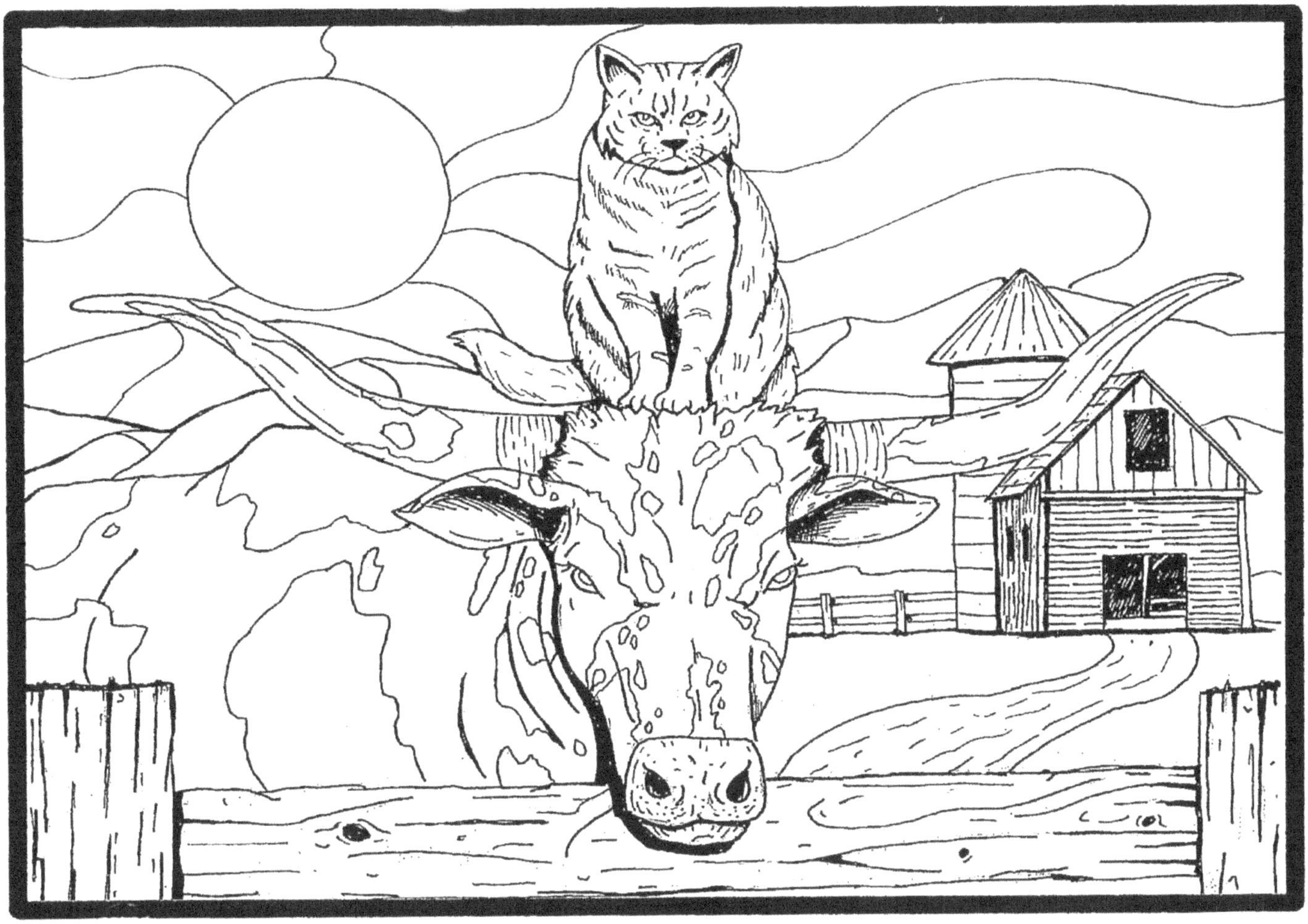

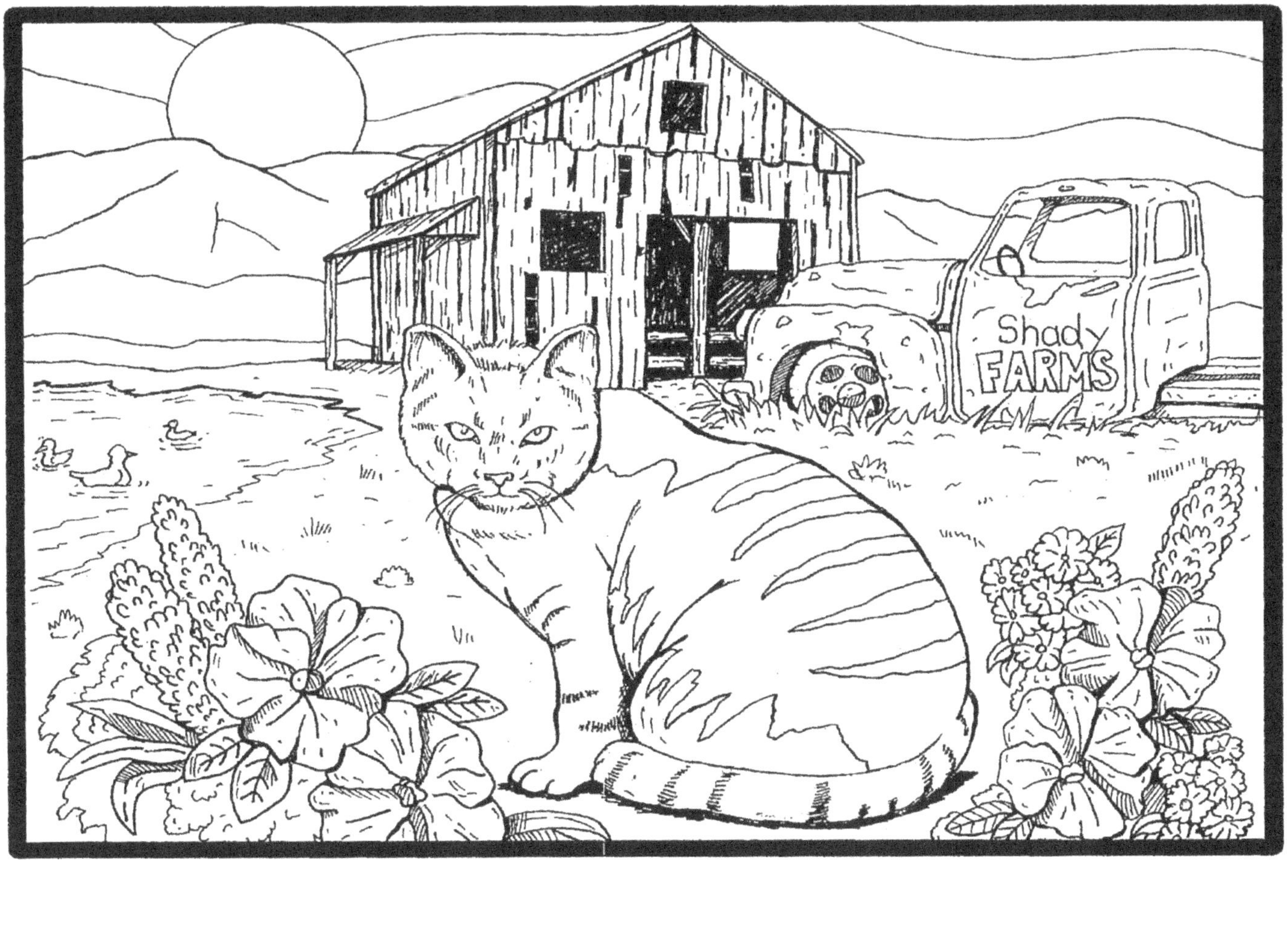

Shady FARMS

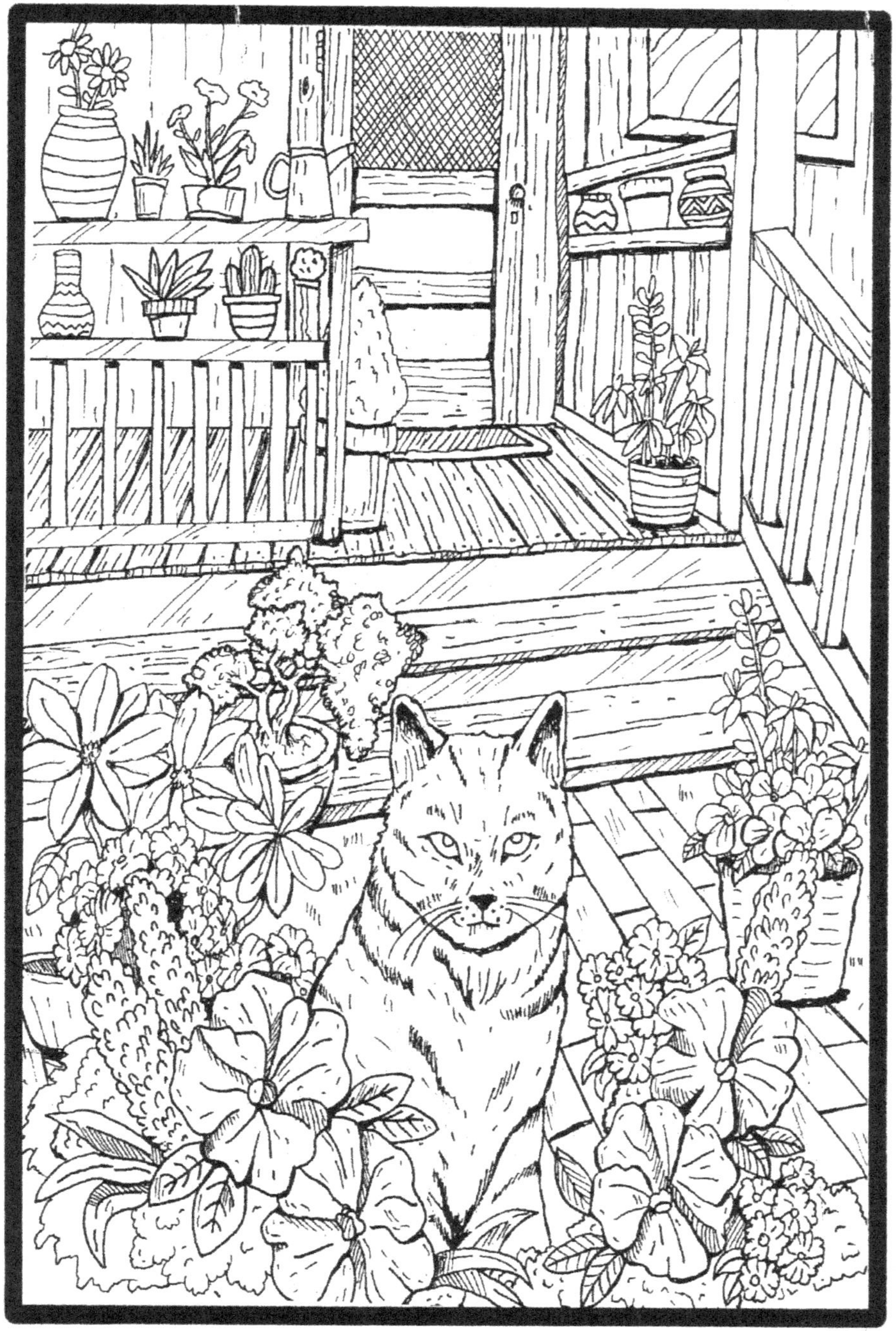

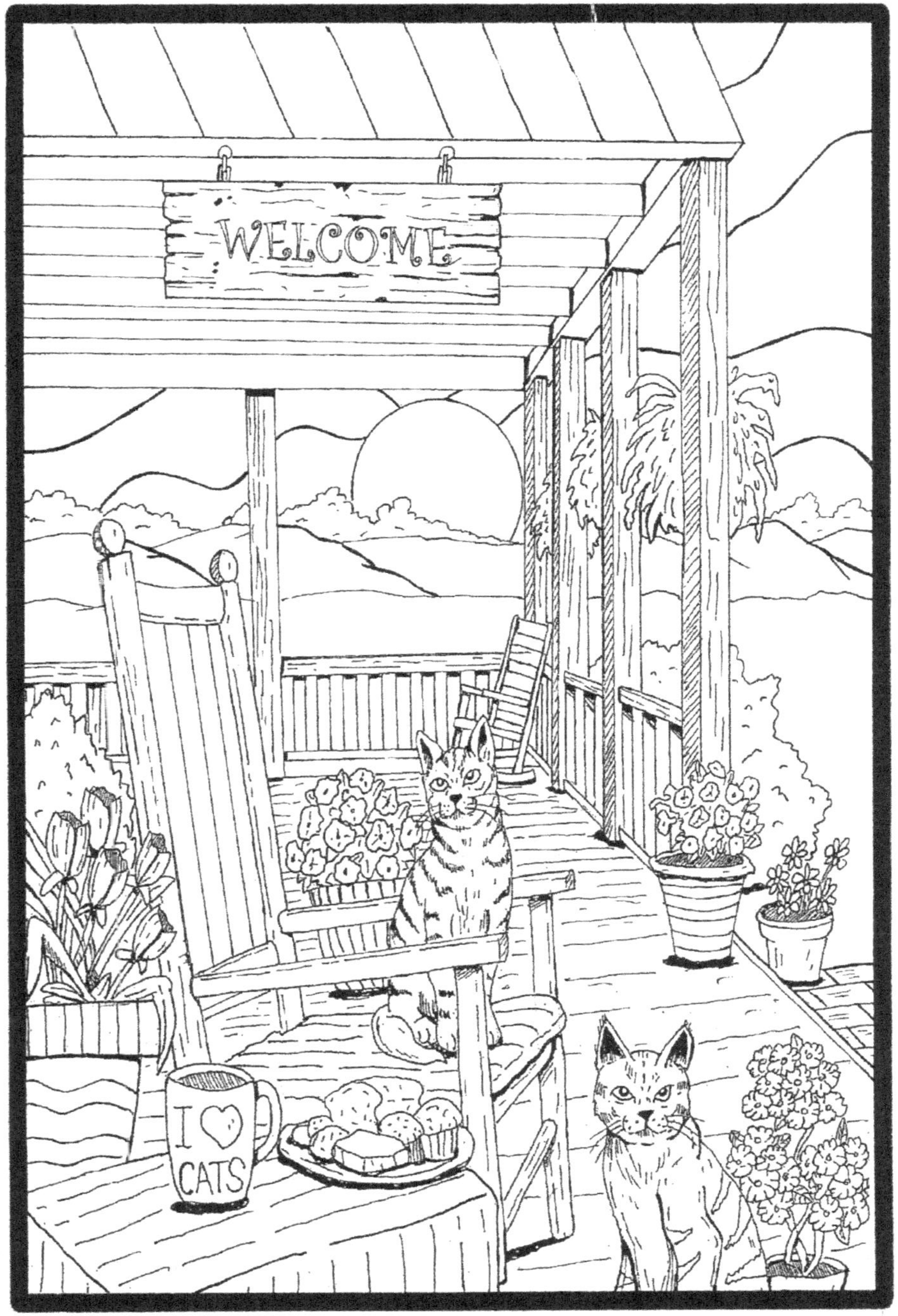
WELCOME
I ♥ CATS

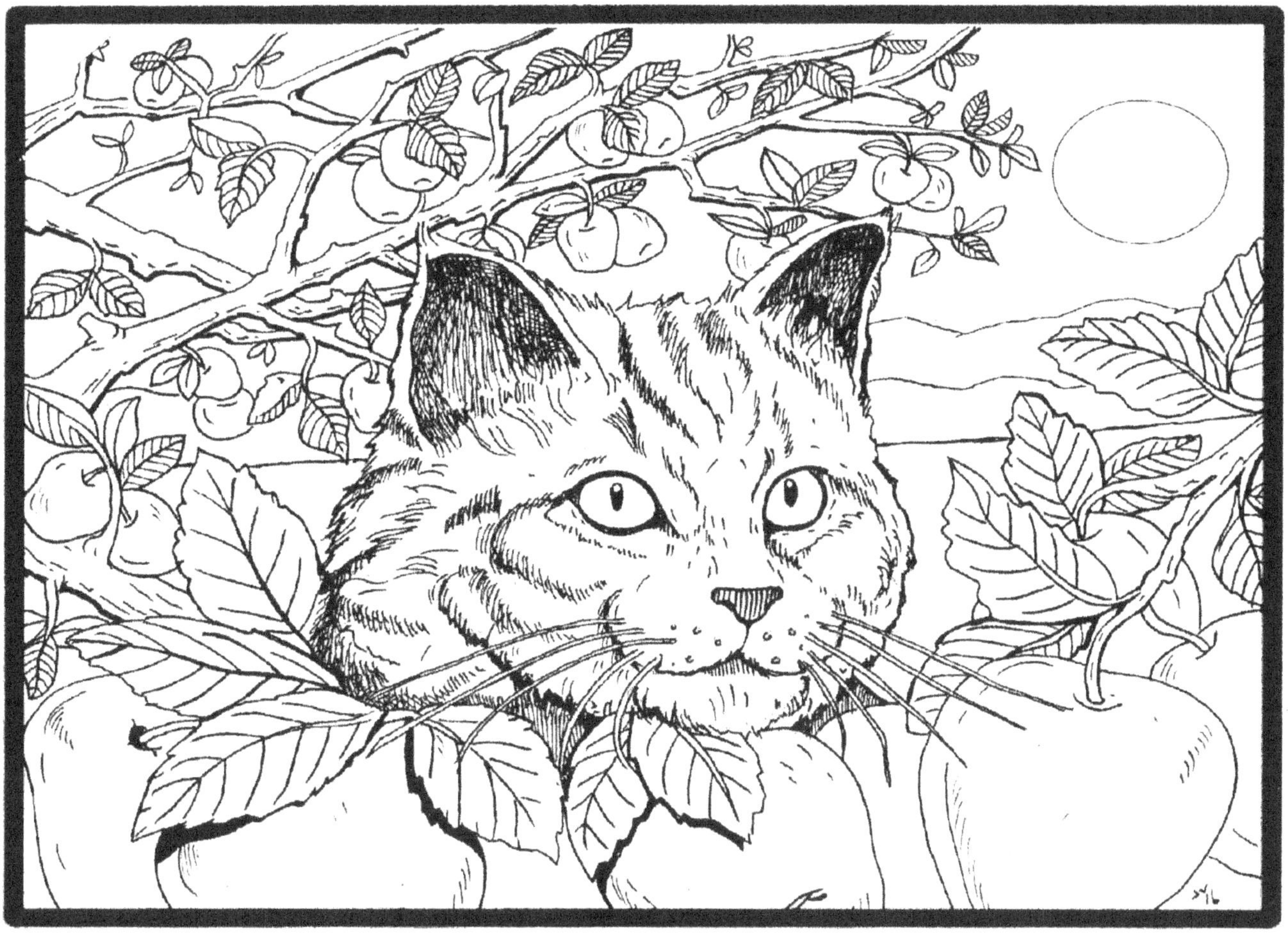

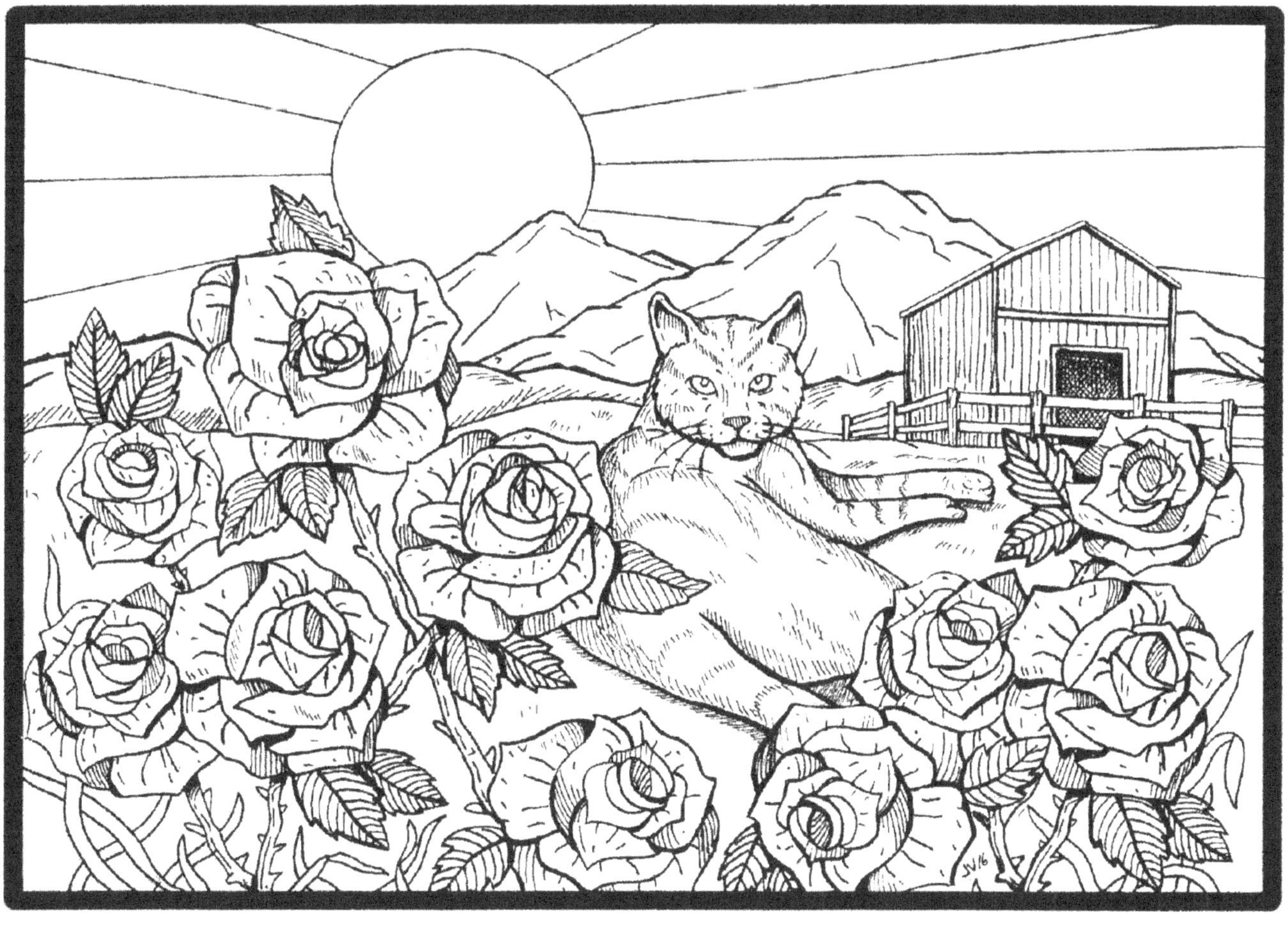

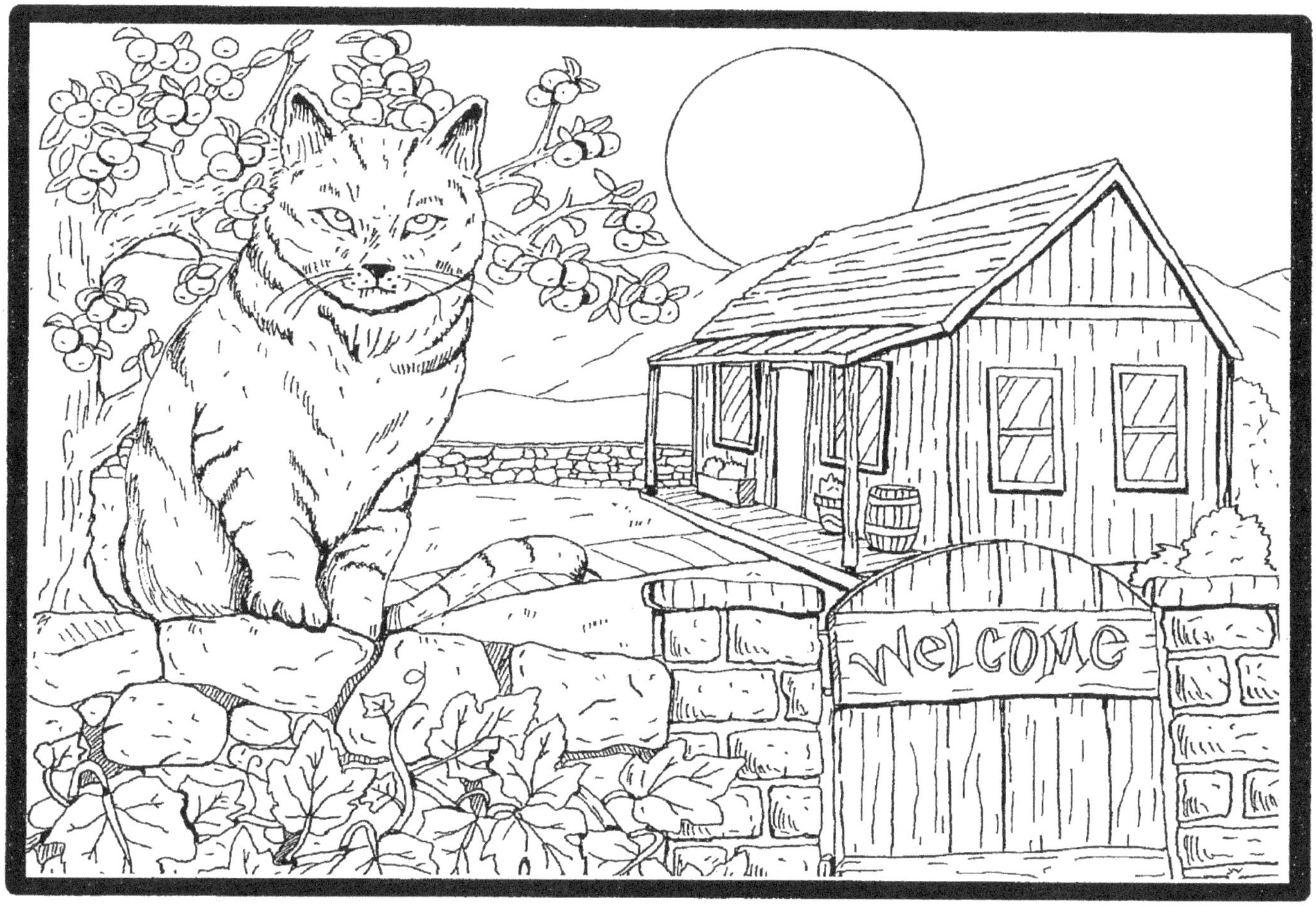
WELCOME

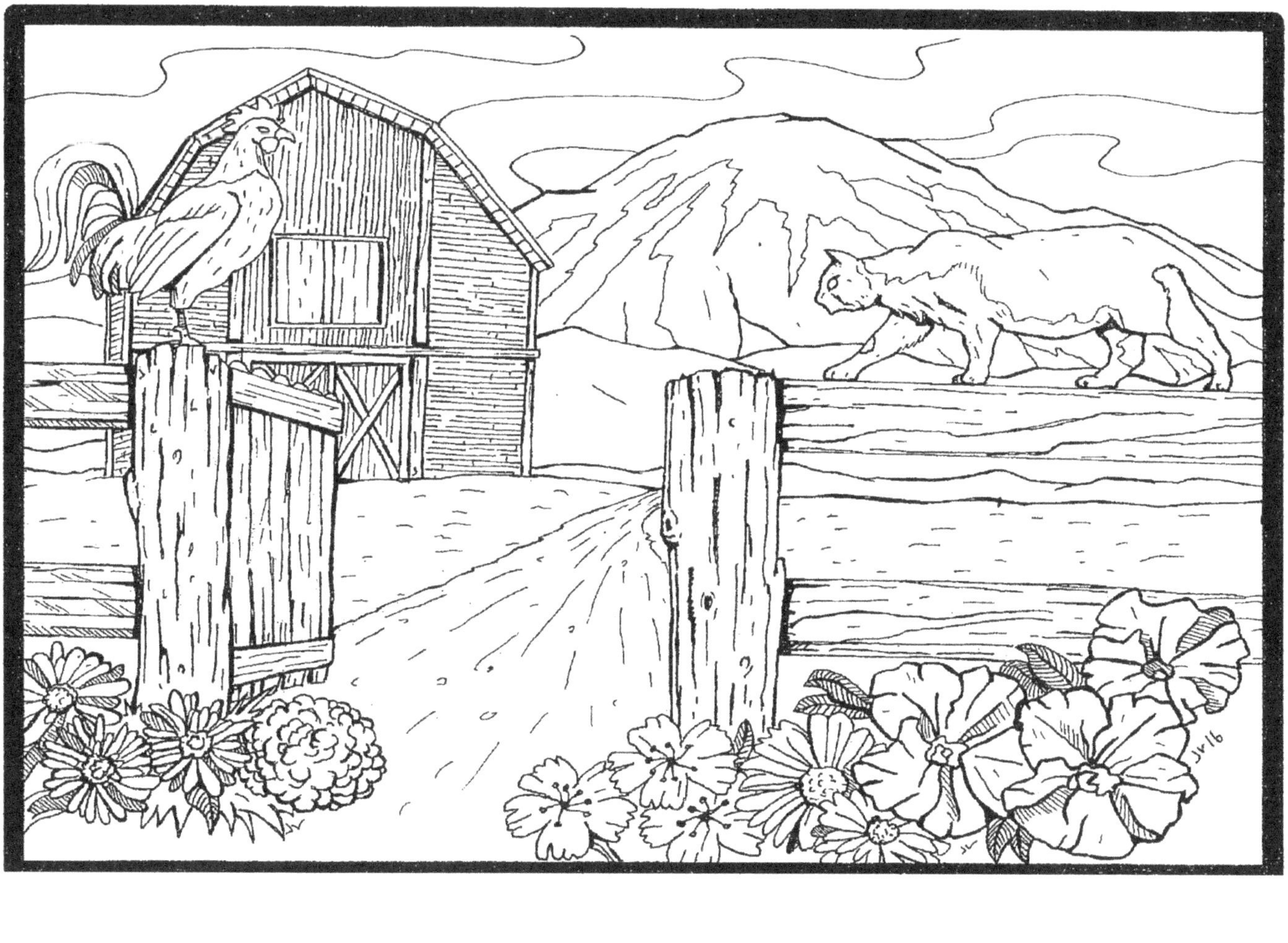

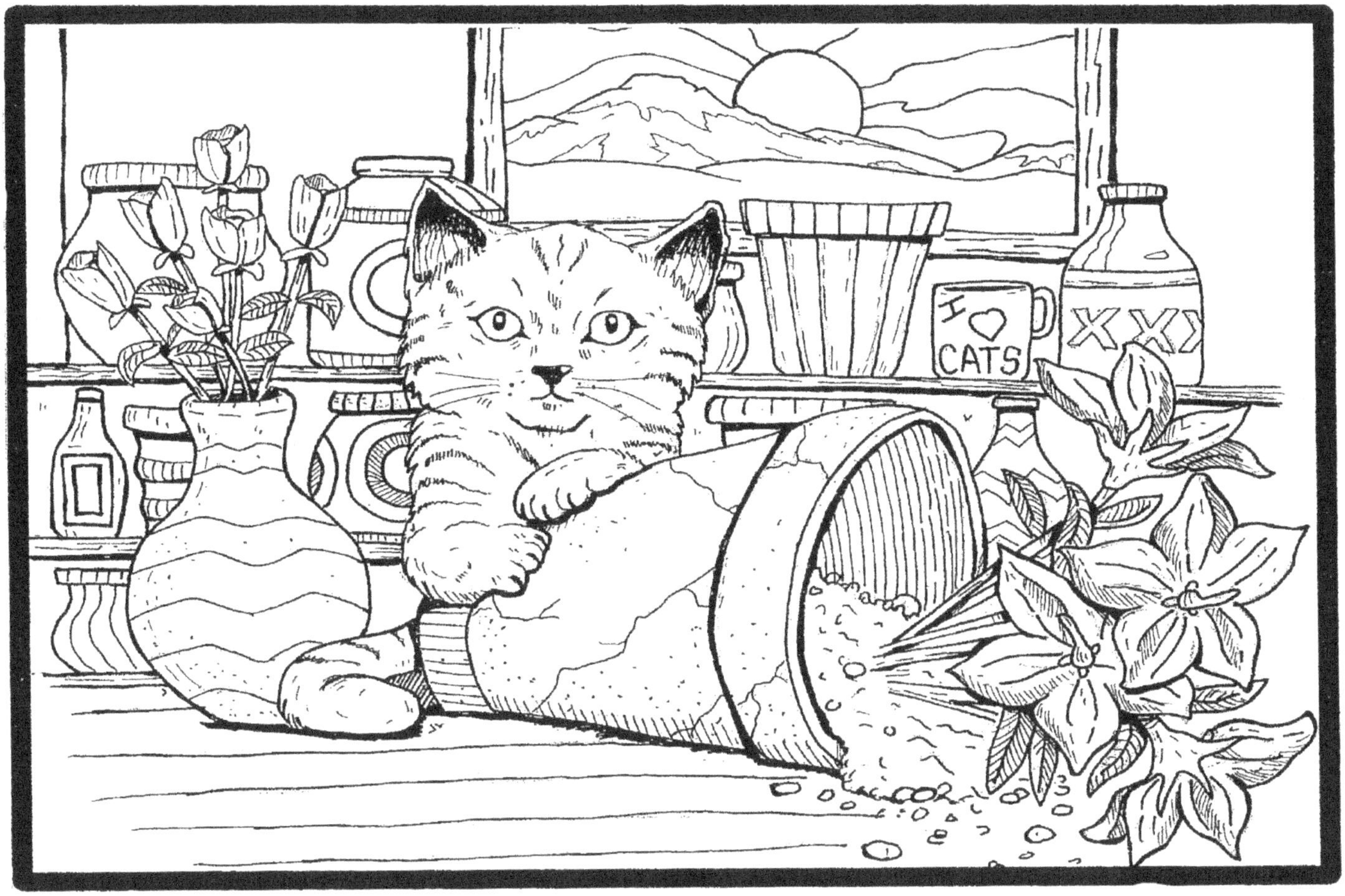
I ♥ CATS
XXX

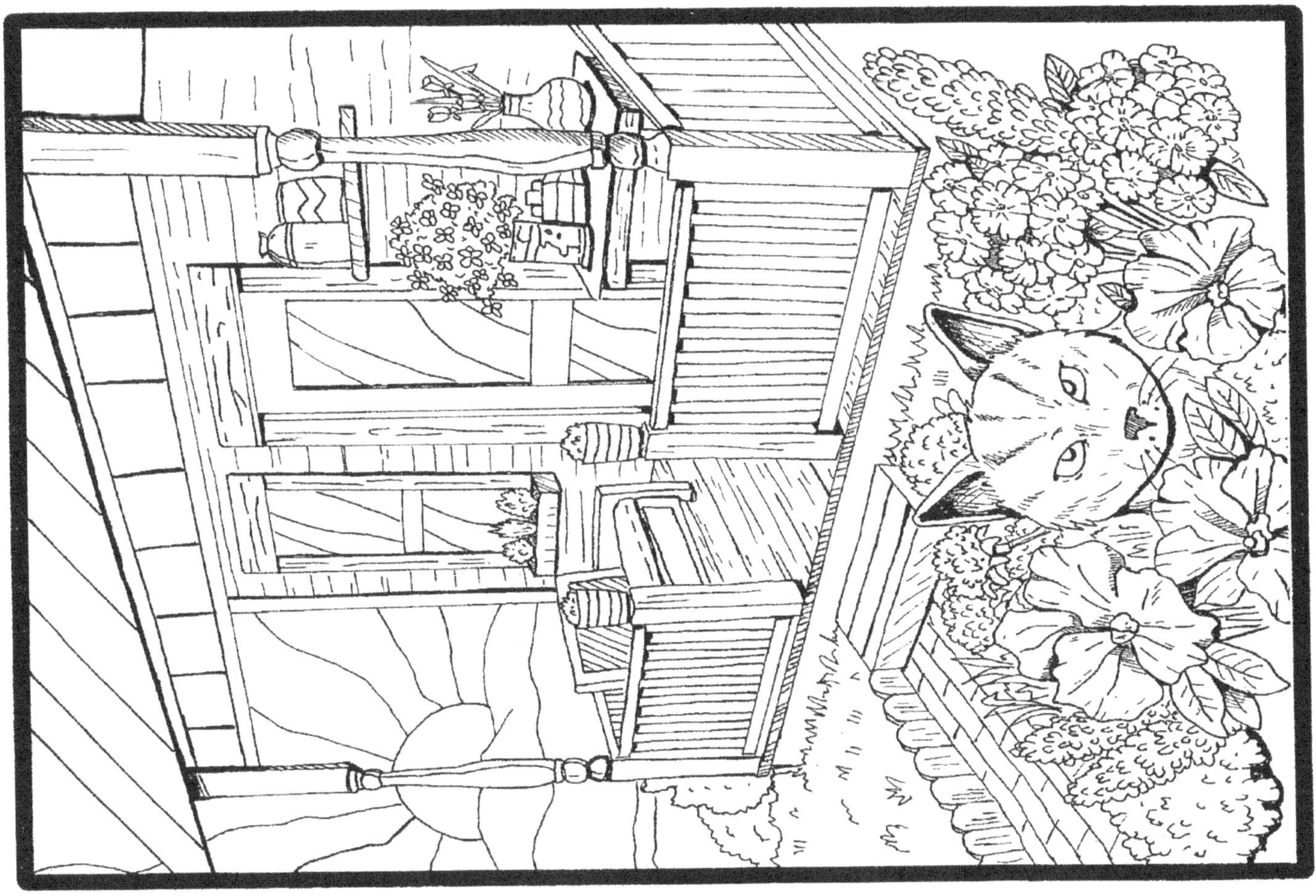

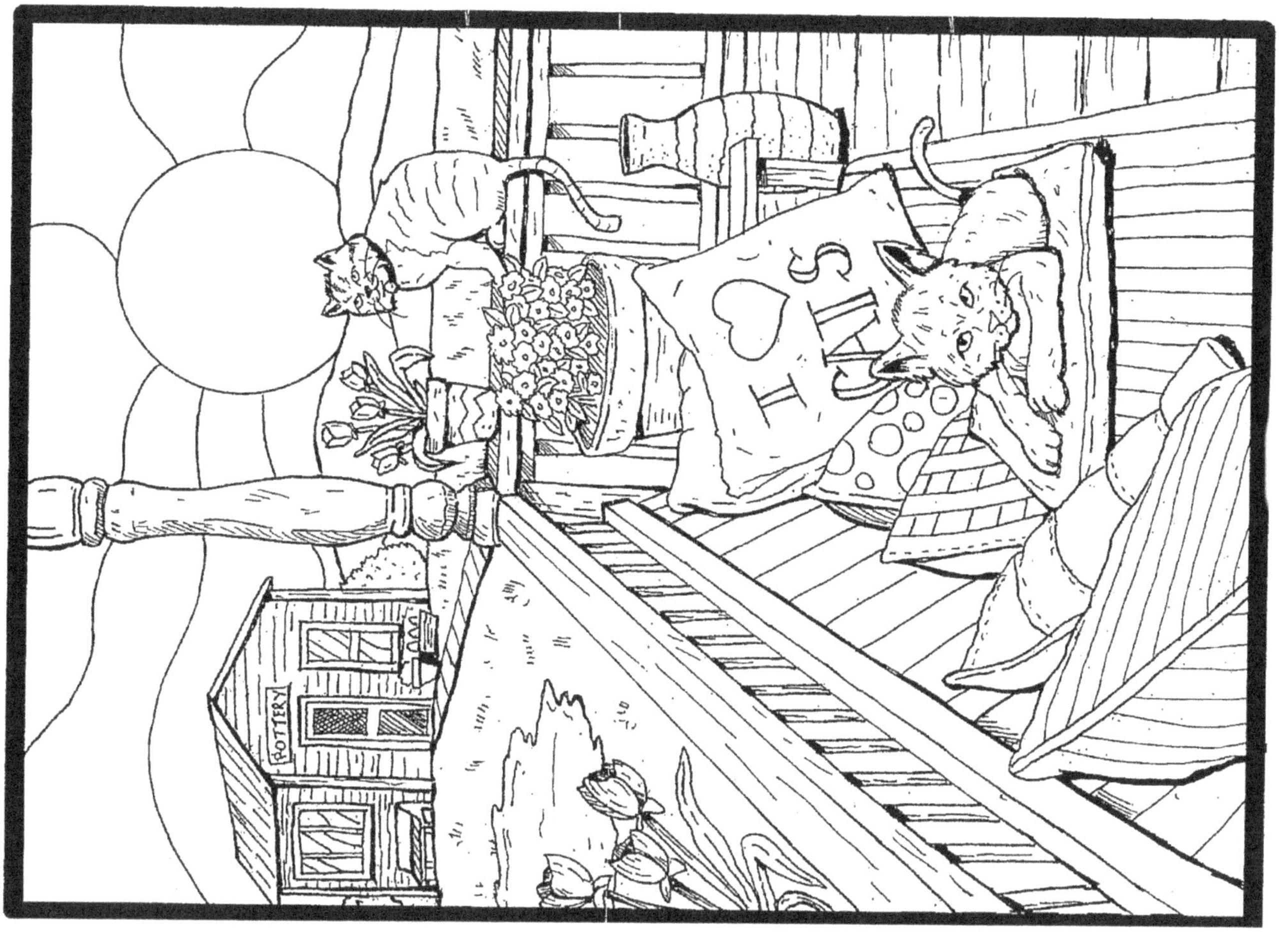
POTTERY

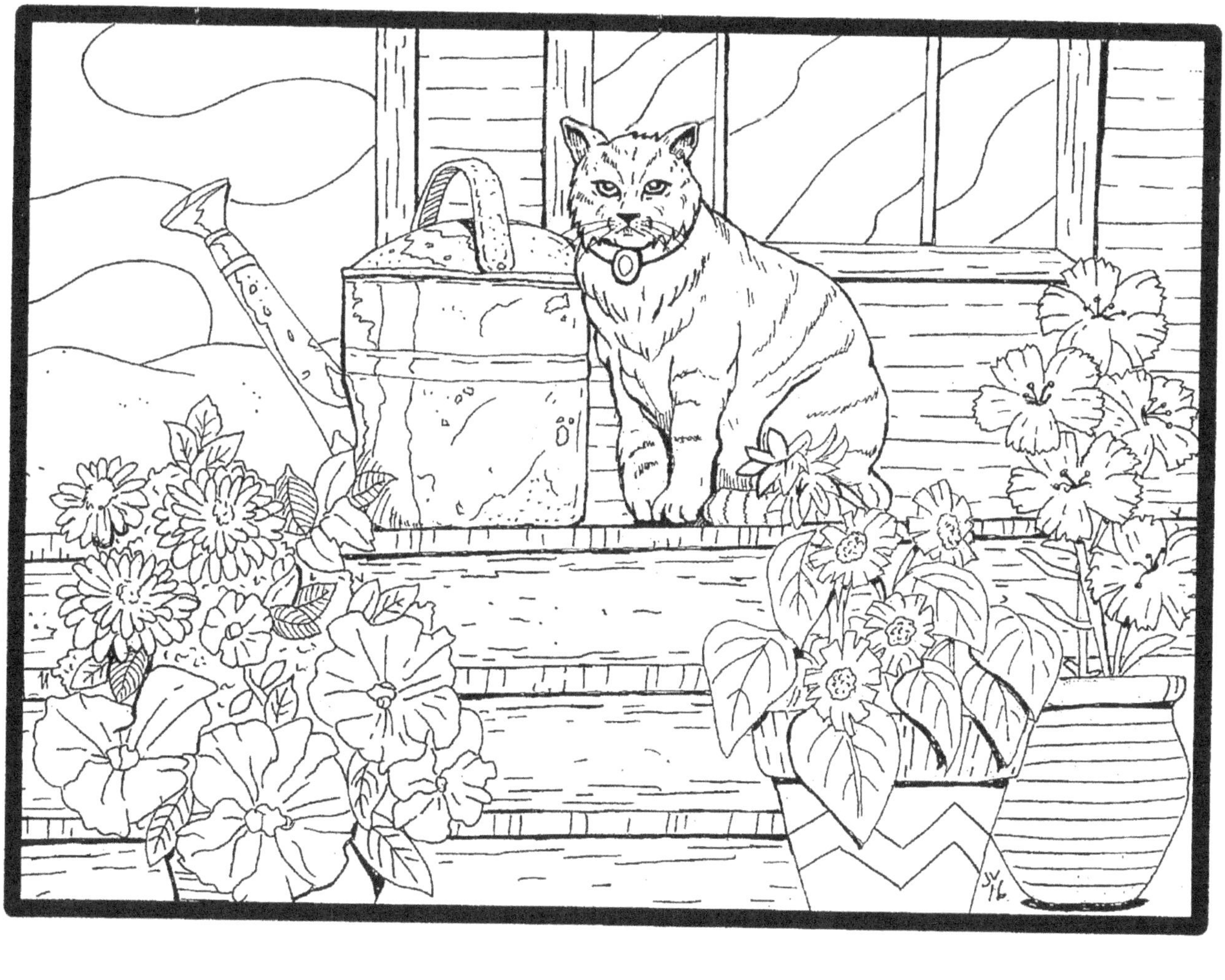

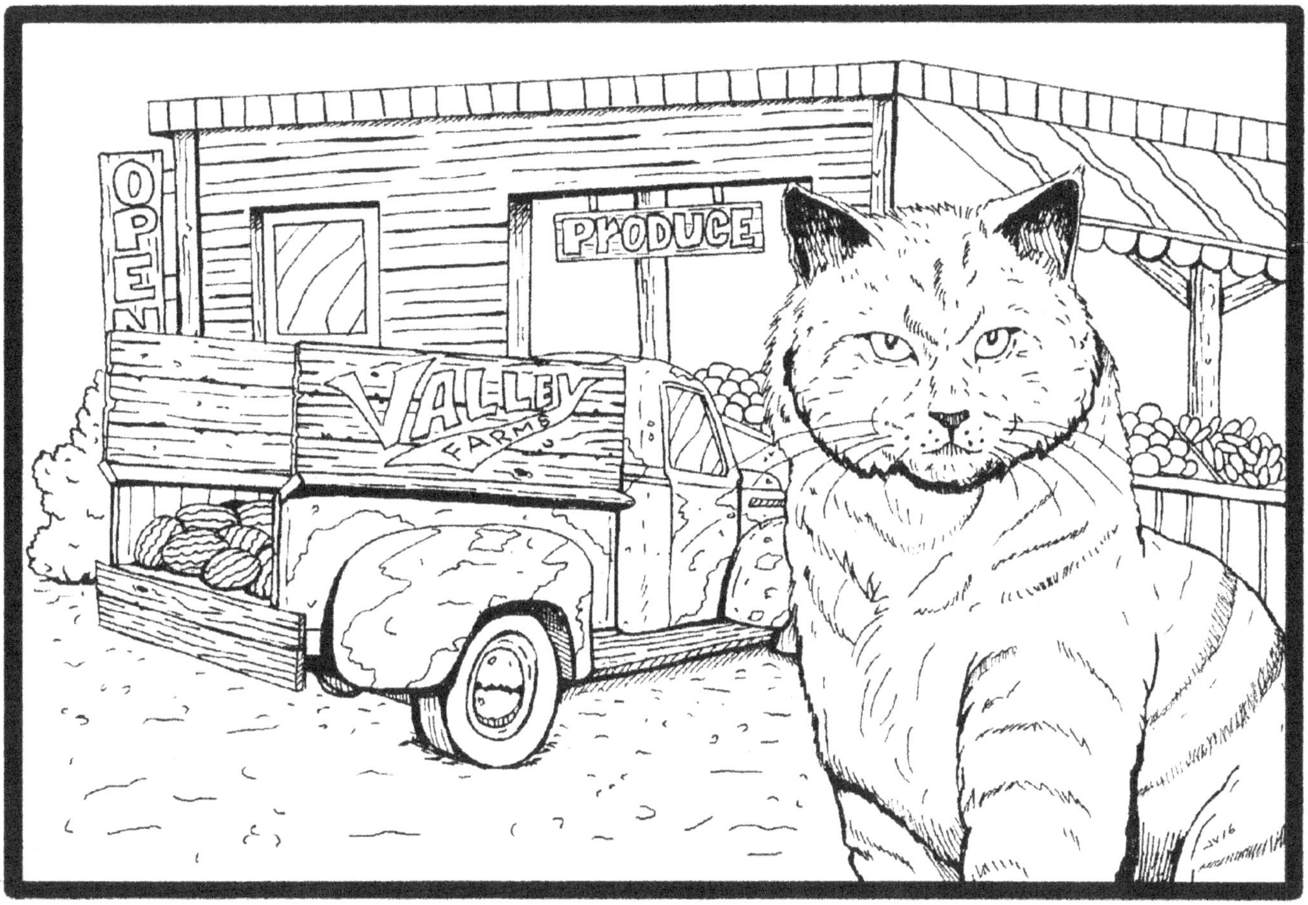
OPEN
PRODUCE
VALLEY
FARMS

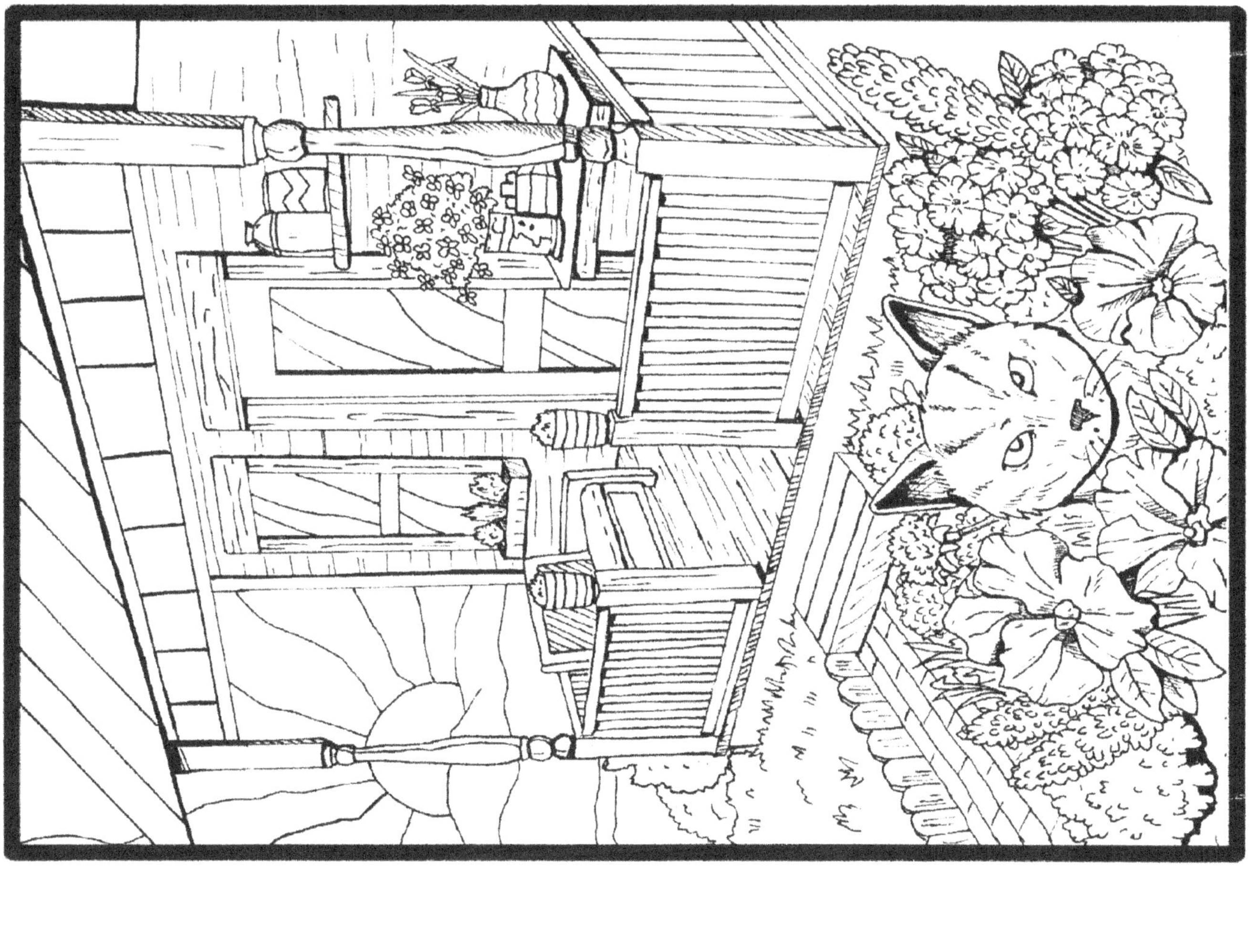

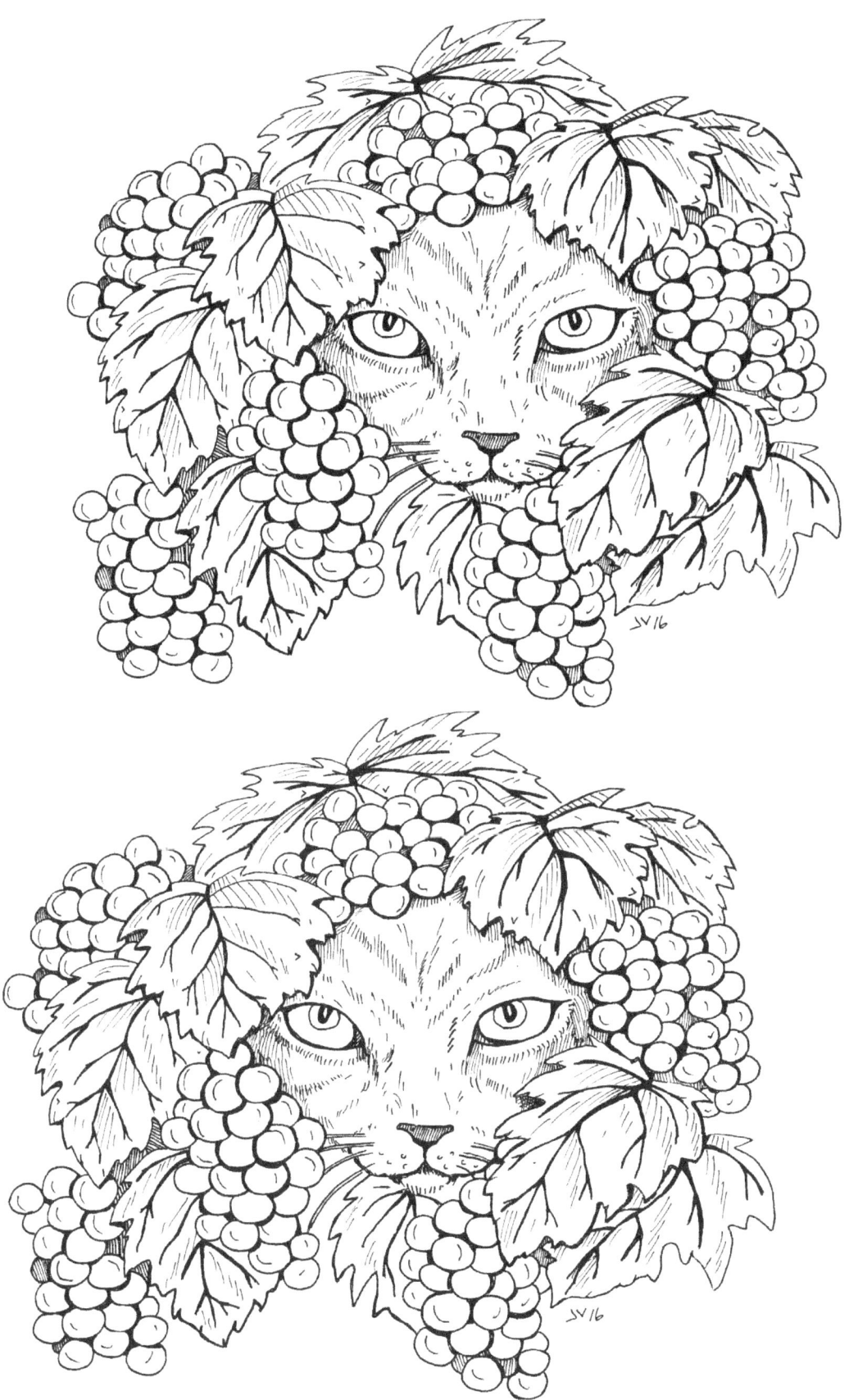

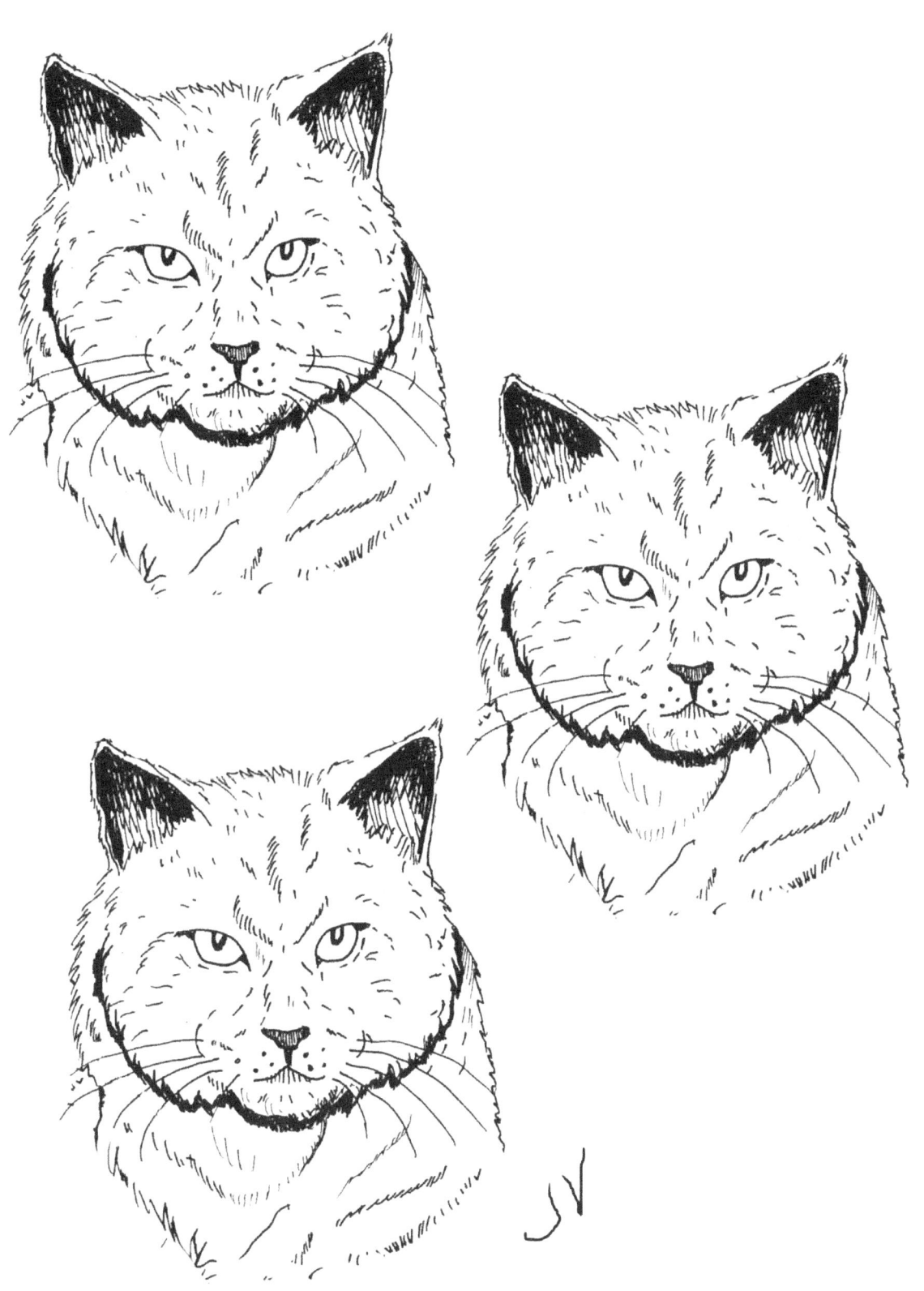

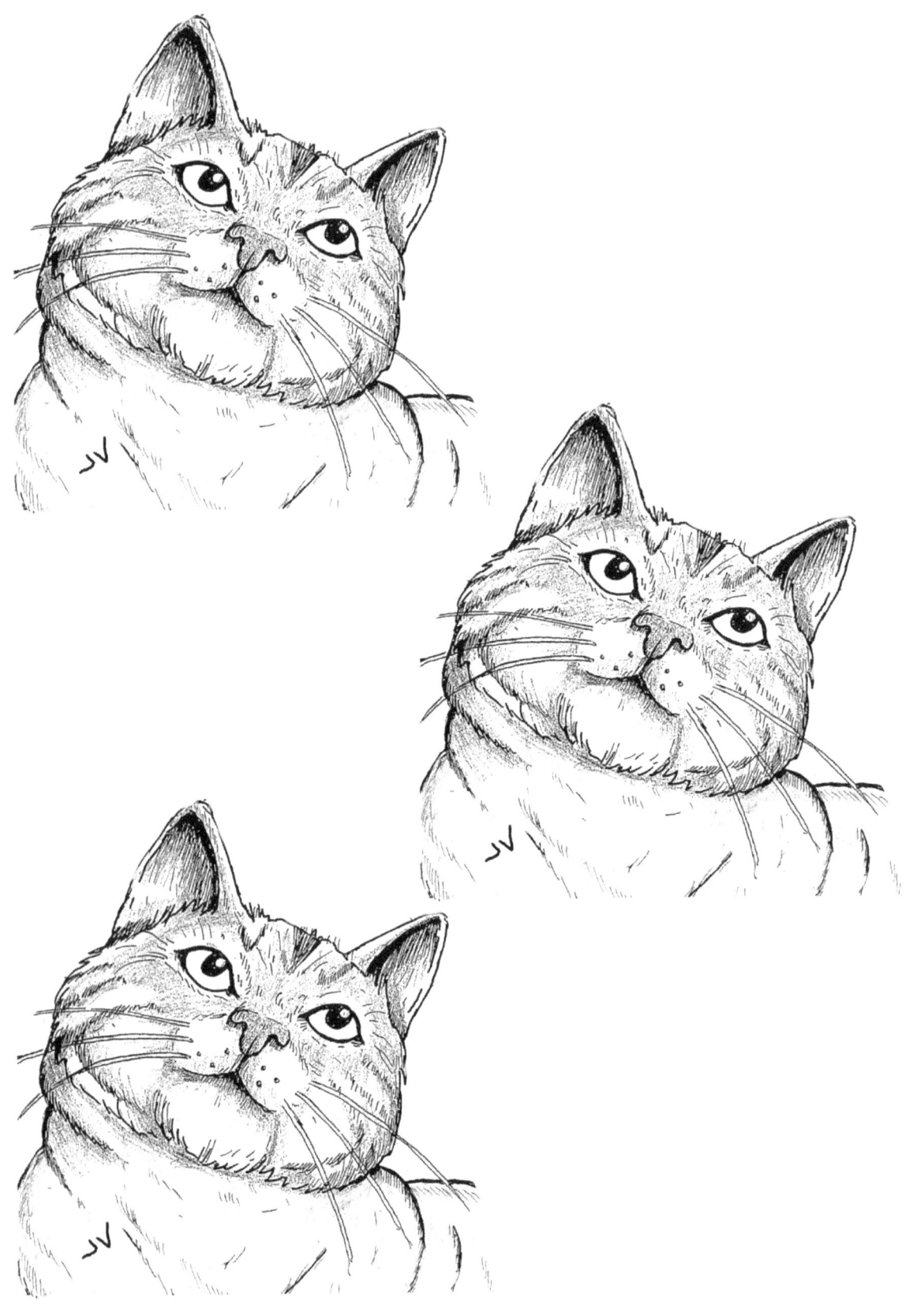

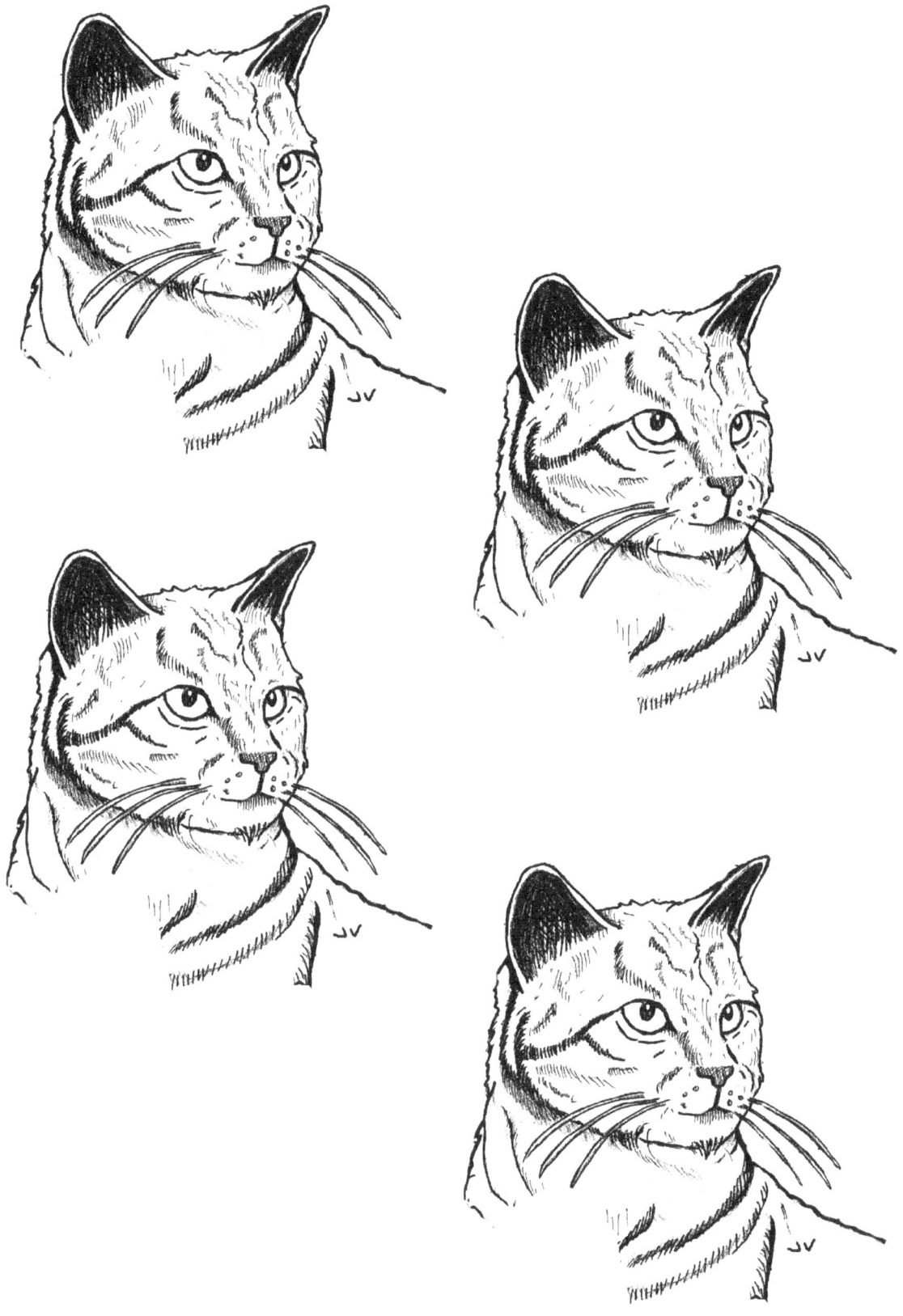

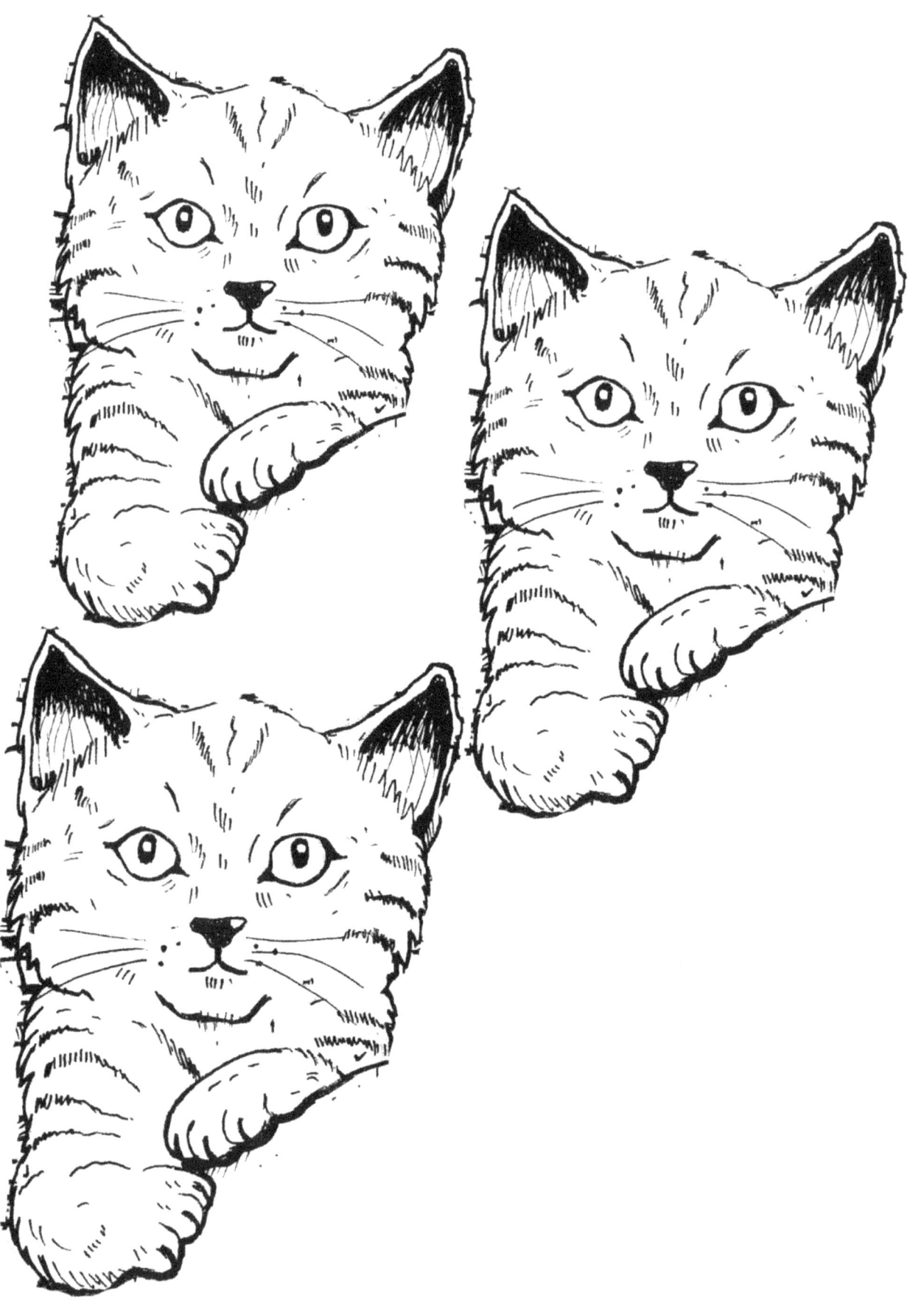

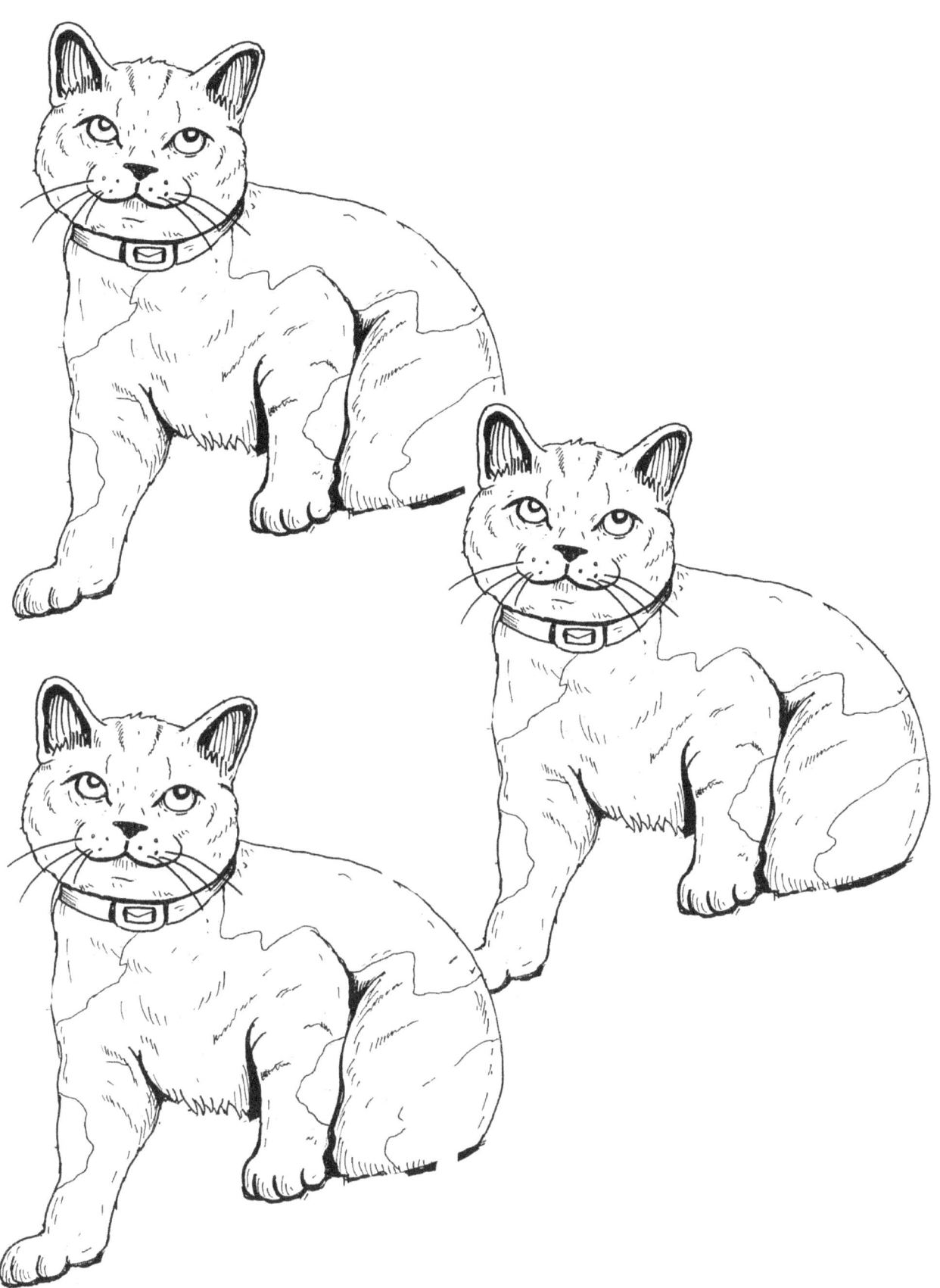

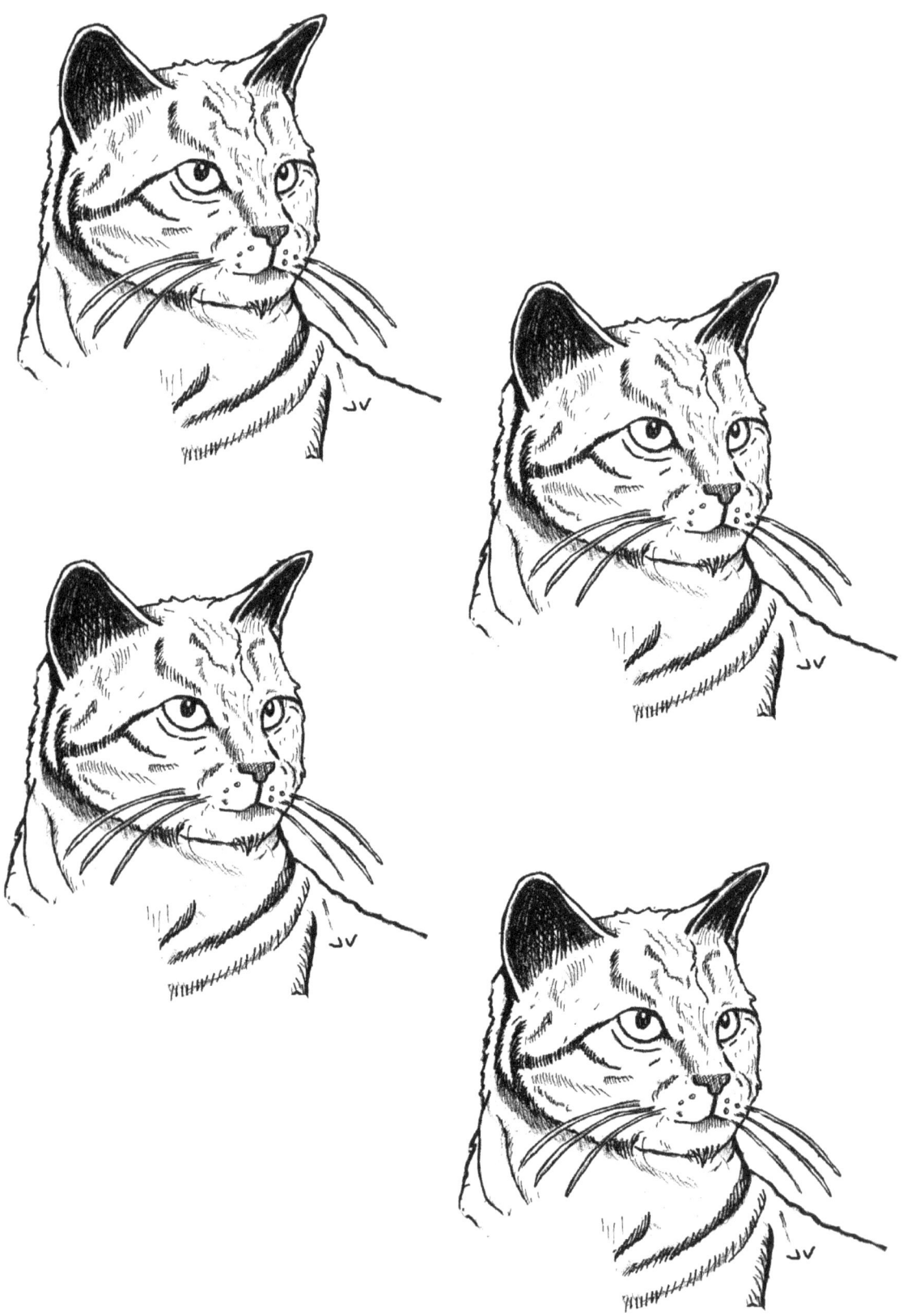

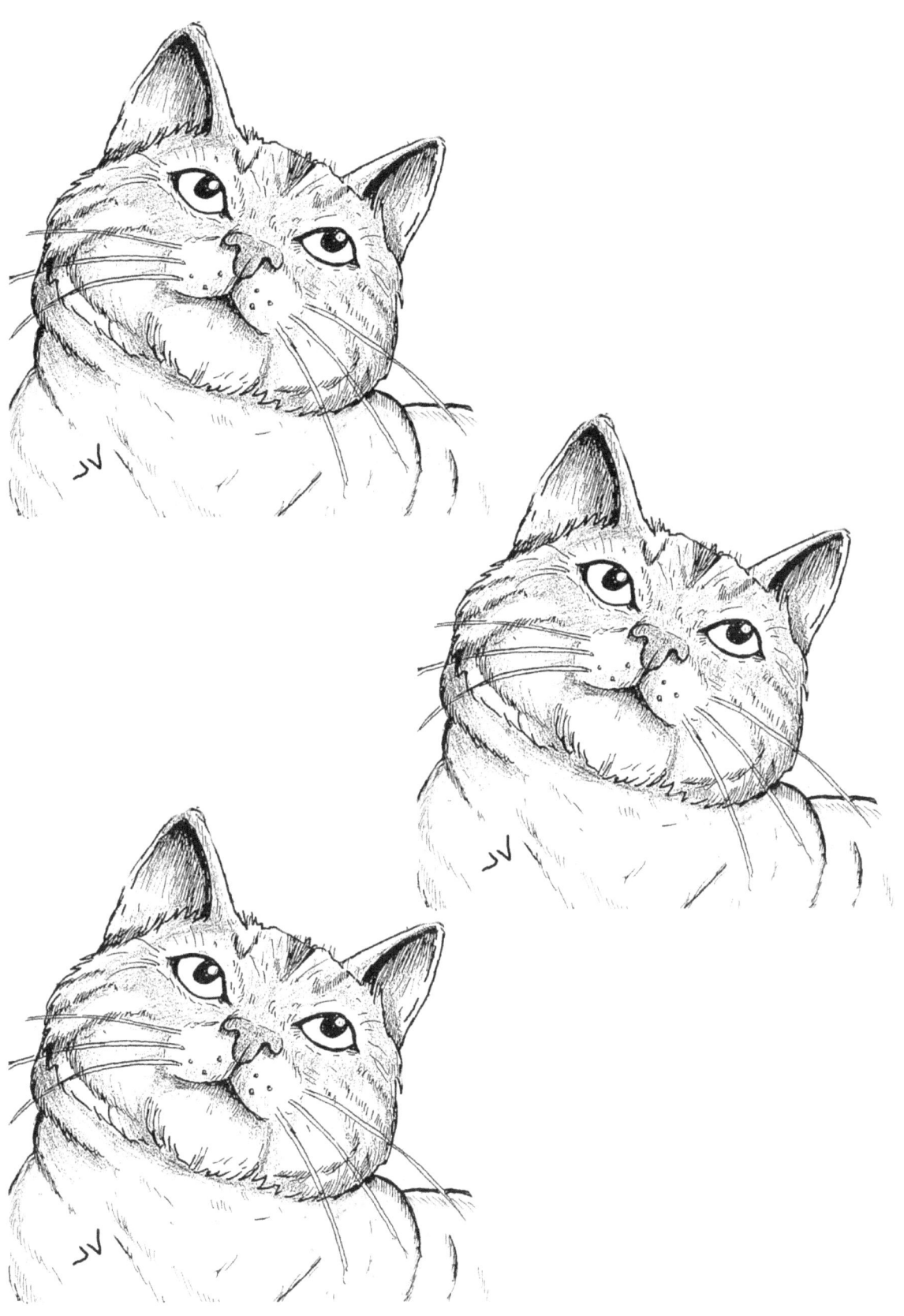

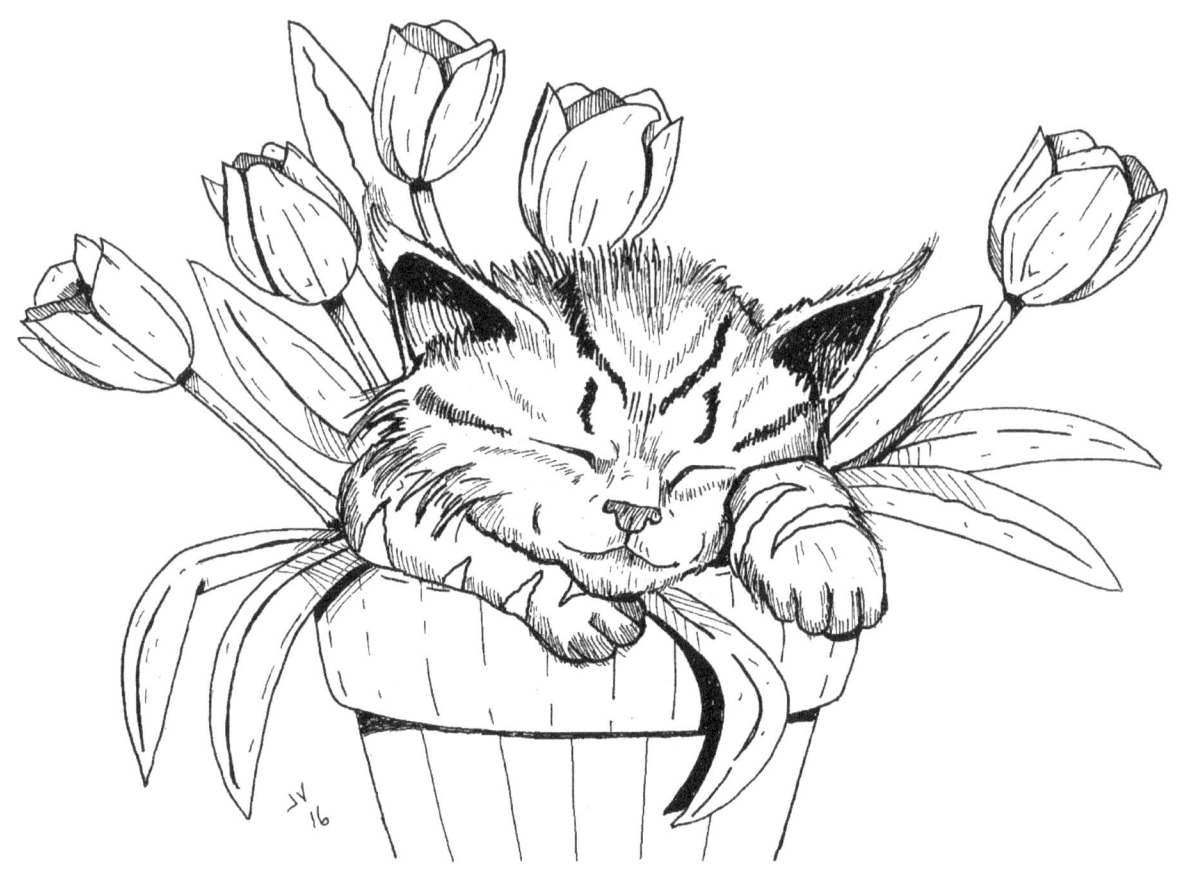

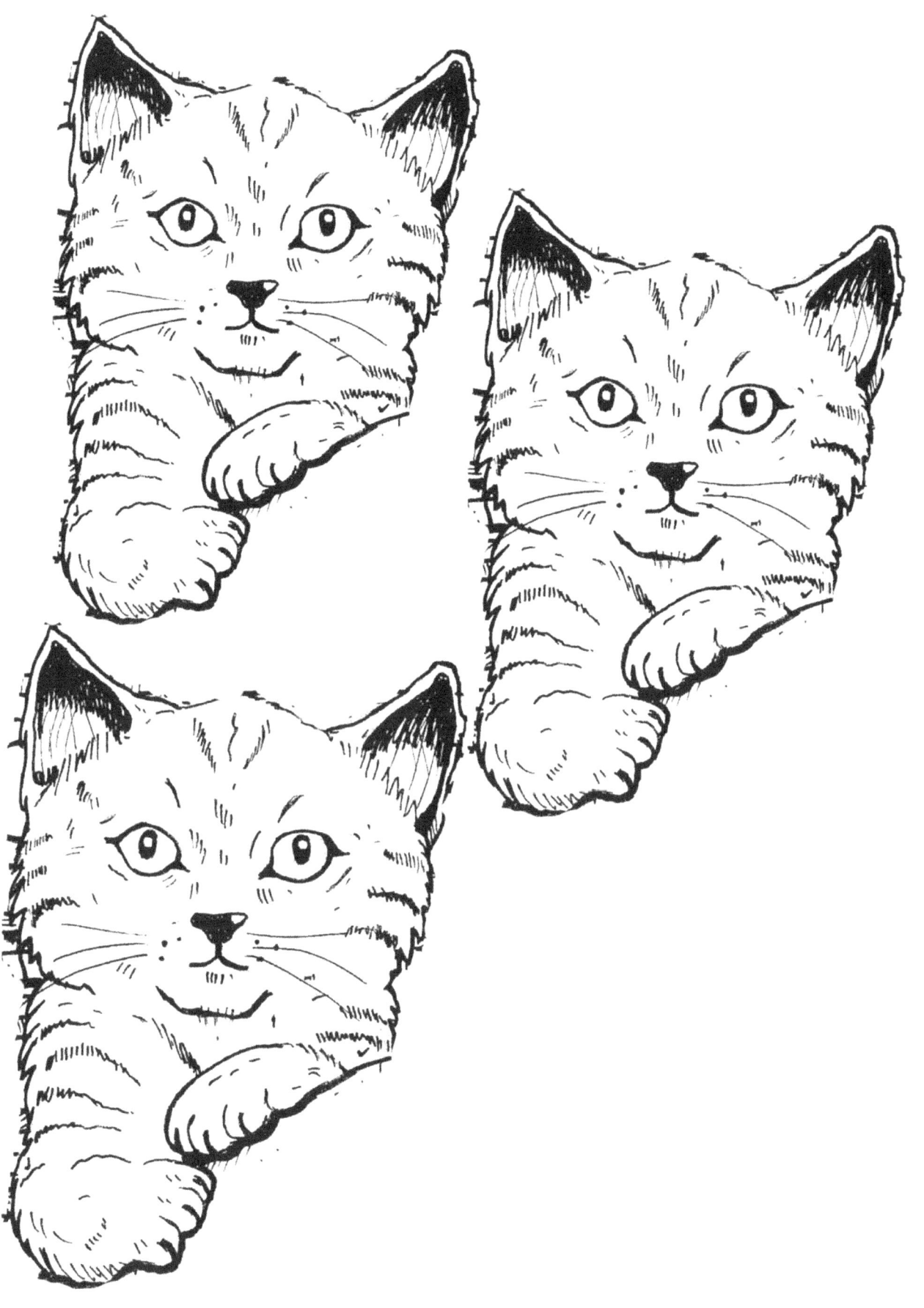

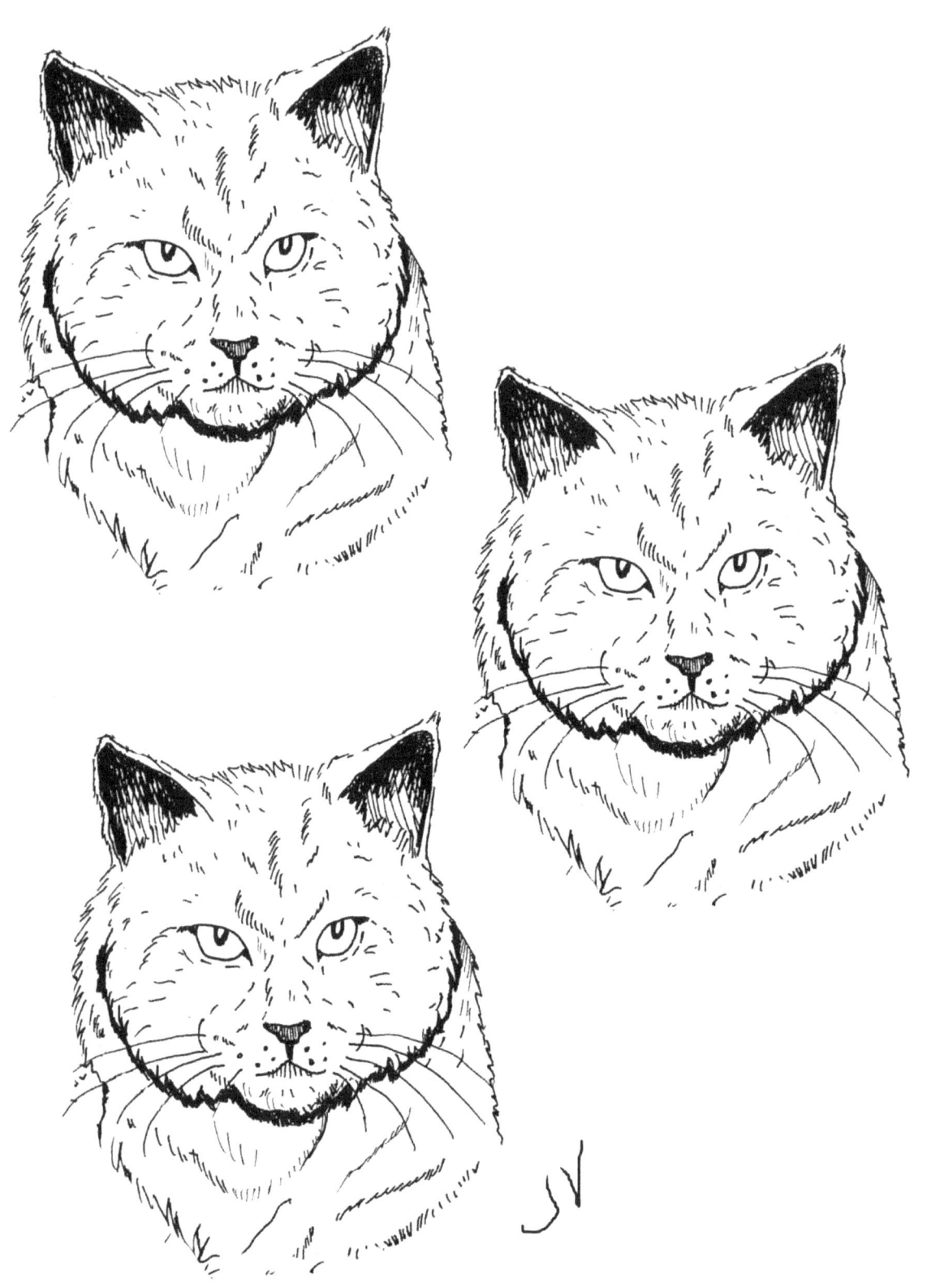

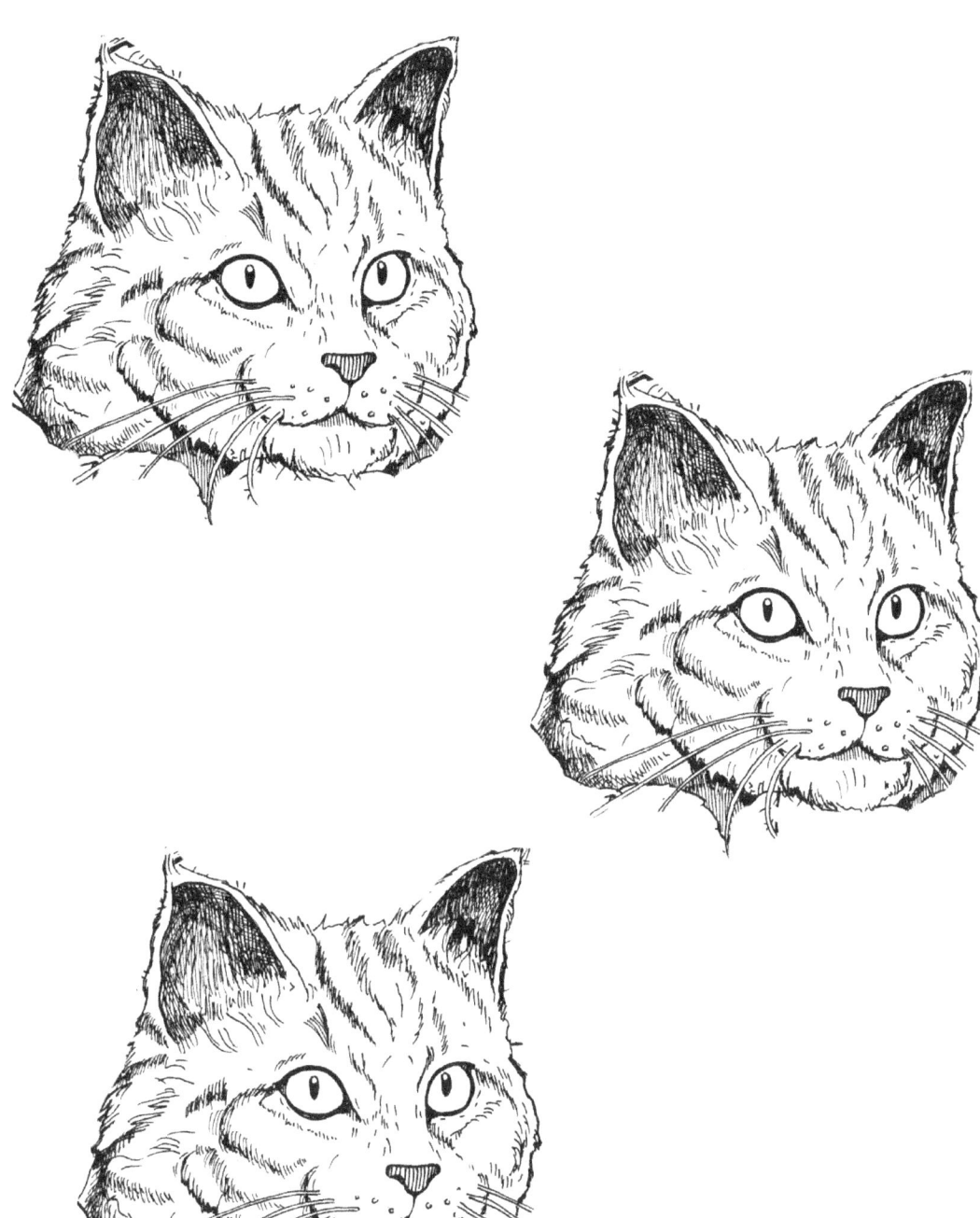

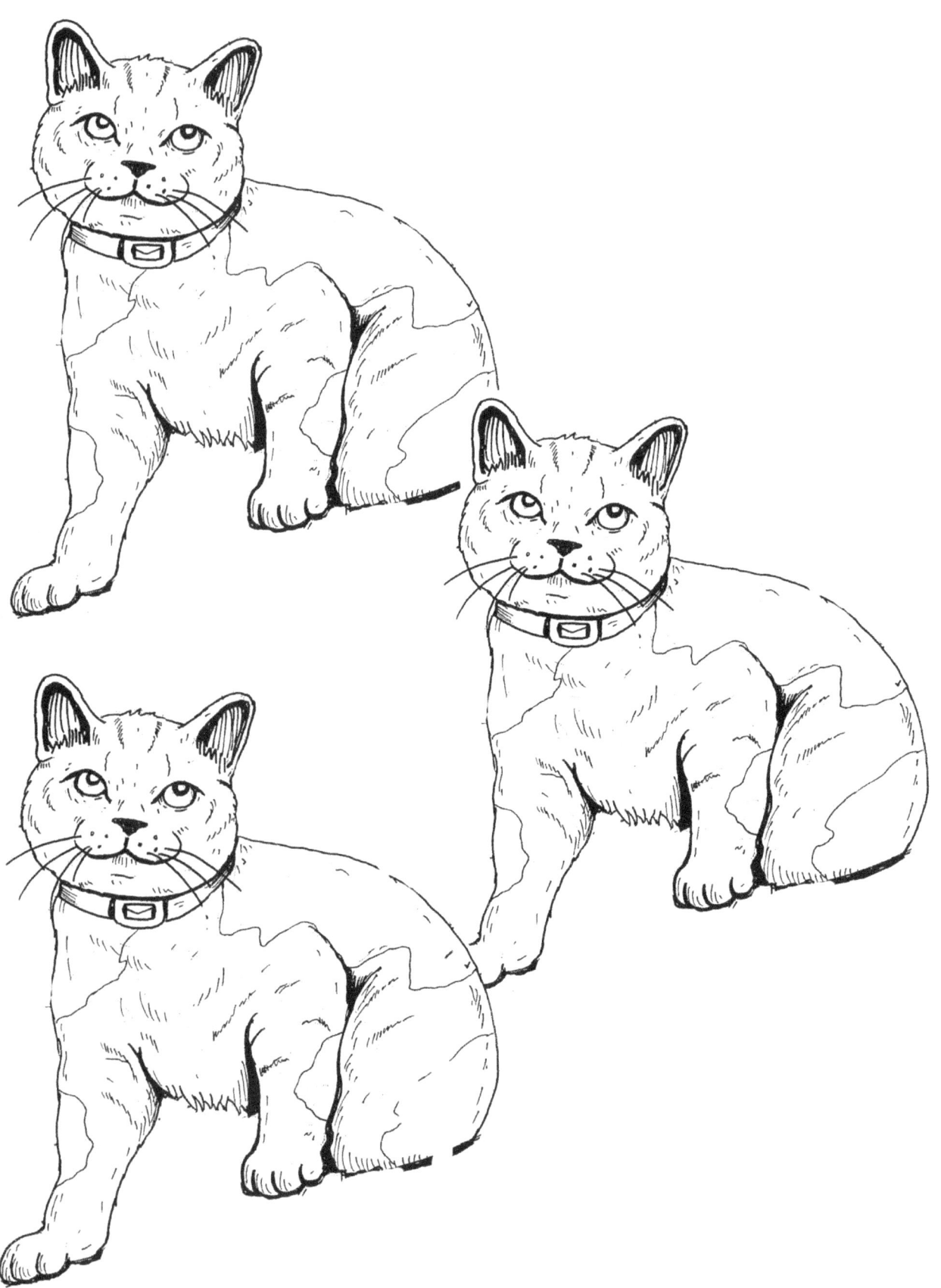

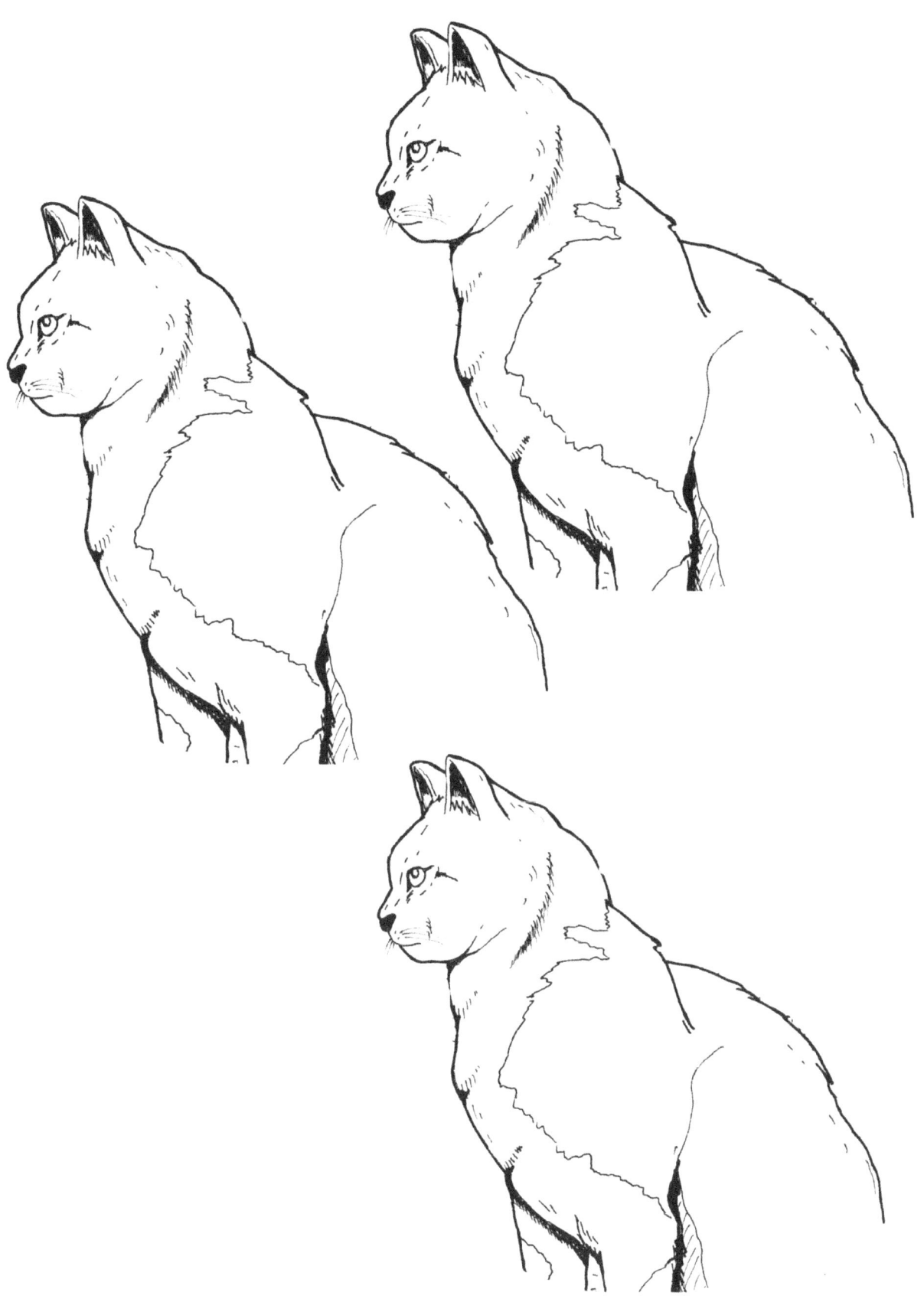

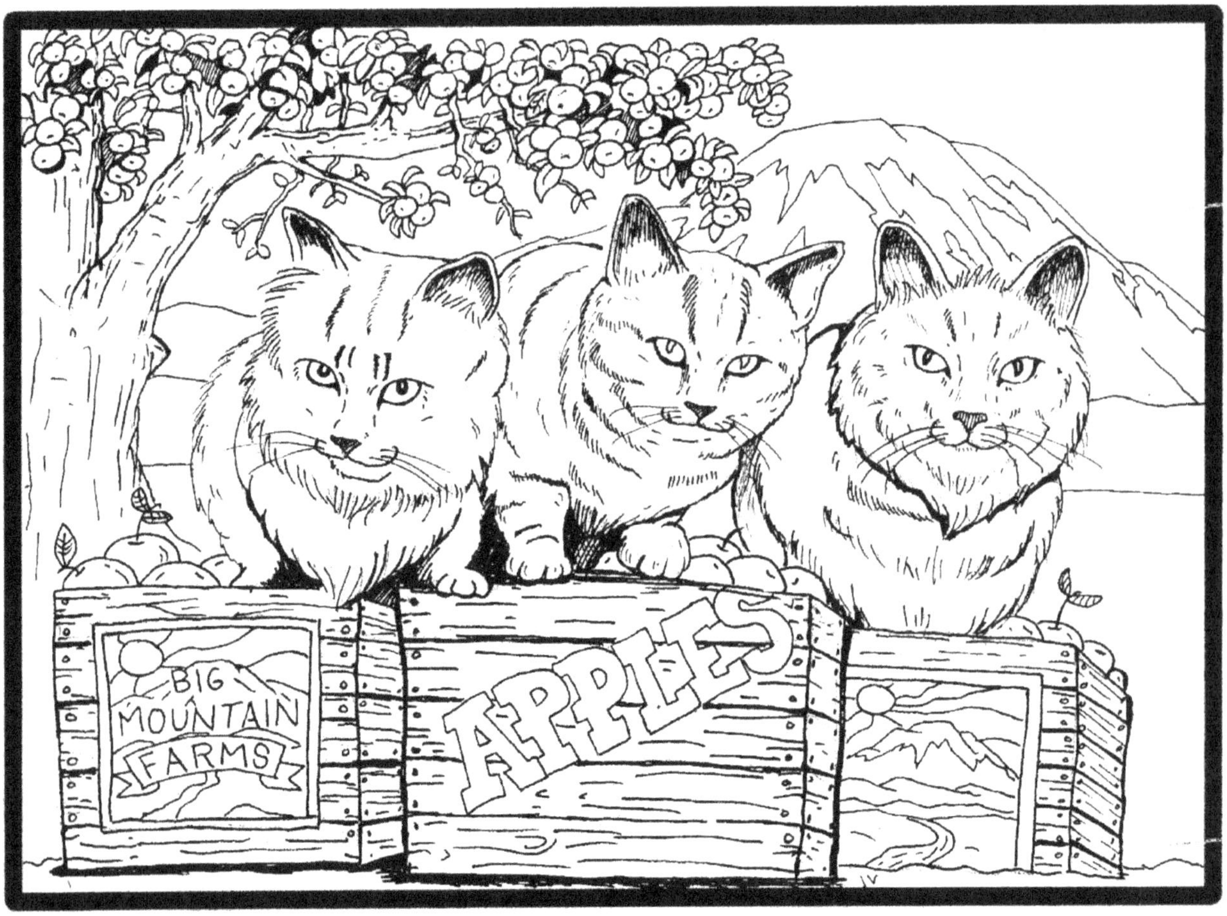

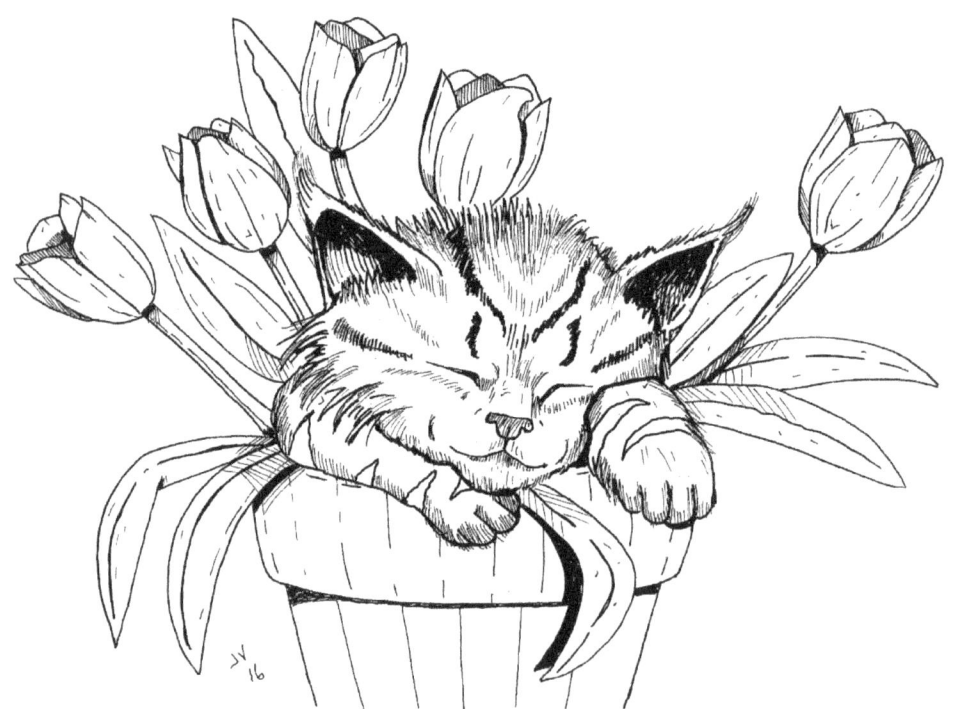

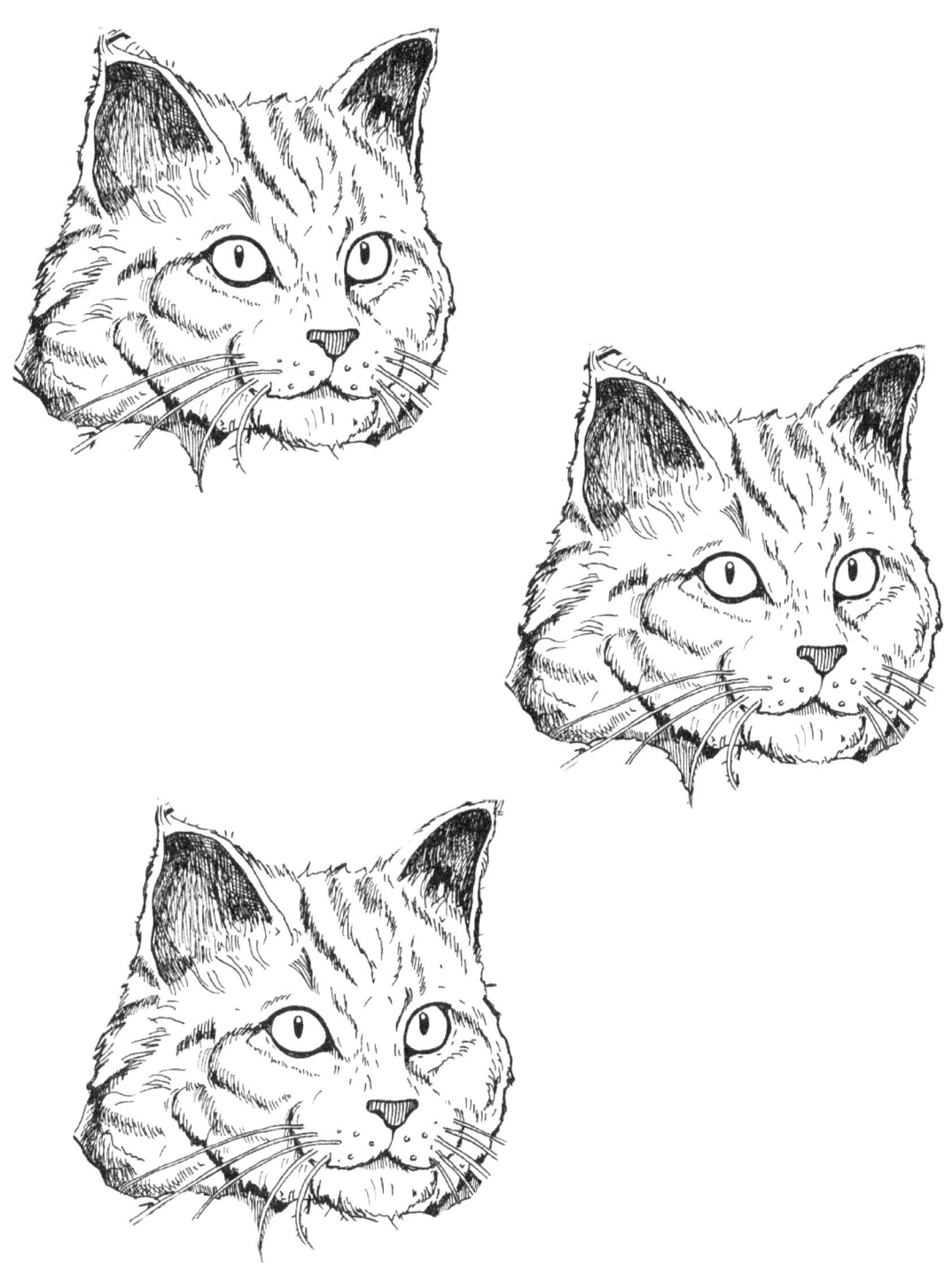

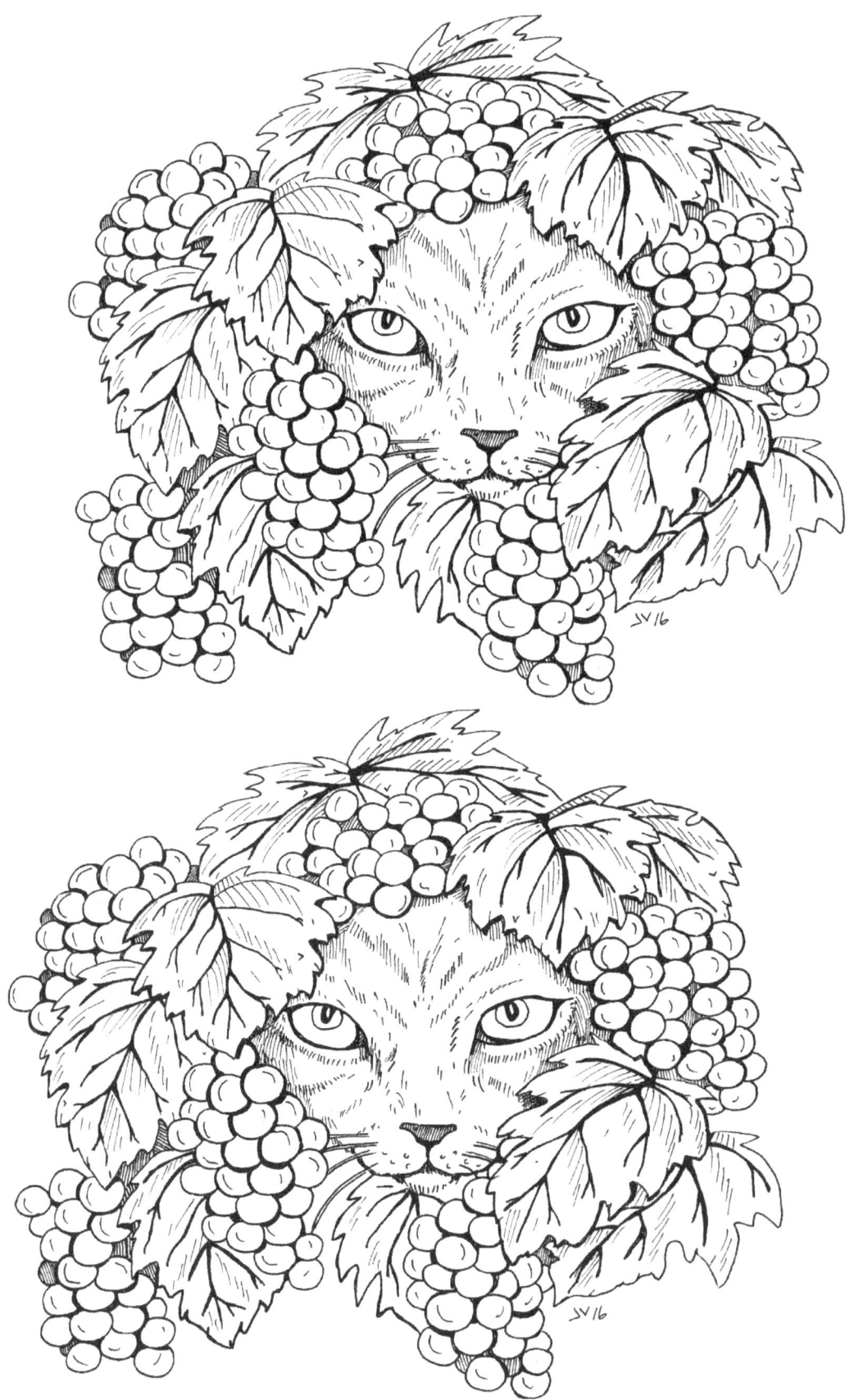

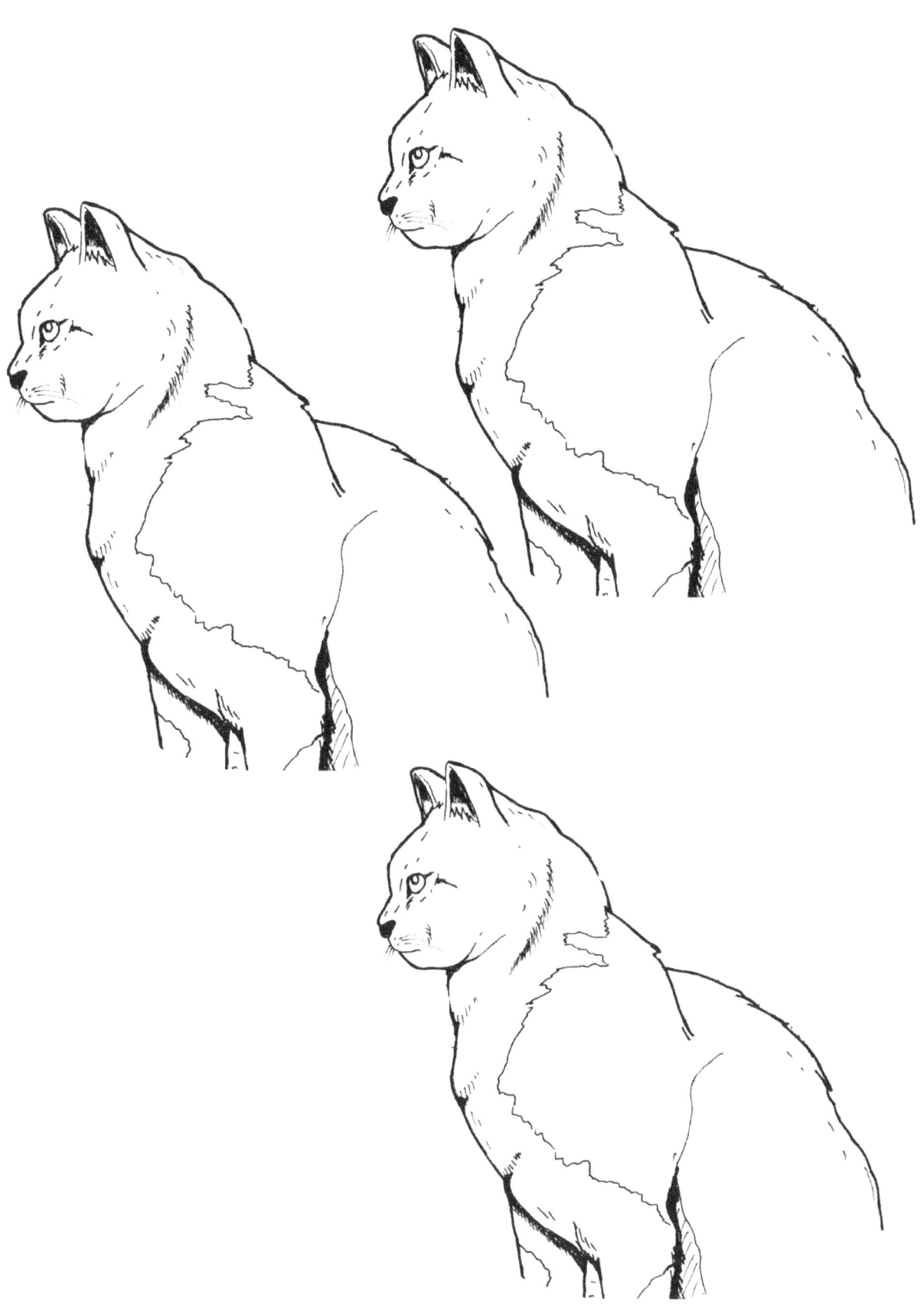

Thank you for your support…..keep coloring and keep creating.

JV

www.ingramcontent.com/pod-product-compliance
Lightning Source LLC
Chambersburg PA
CBHW080719190526
45169CB00006B/2434